Nourishing the Mind

A 6-Week Journey to Overcome Depression and Anxiety

Jerry Clarke

TABLE OF CONTENTS

PART 1: NOURISHING YOUR MENTAL WELLNESS

Introduction:

In a world where our days are woven with the threads of stress, uncertainty, and the constant hum of modern life, our minds often find themselves in a tangle of emotions, a maze of thoughts that can lead us down the treacherous path of depression and anxiety. It's a journey many of us have embarked upon, but what if there was a way to navigate this labyrinth with resilience, to chart a course towards mental well-being that is both scientifically grounded and profoundly transformative?

Ladies and gentlemen, welcome to the remarkable odyssey that is "Nourishing the Mind: A 6-Week Journey to Overcome Depression and Anxiety." This book is not merely a collection of words on pages; it's a lantern that lights the way through the darkness of mental health struggles, a compass pointing towards a realm of vitality, peace, and renewed spirit.

Imagine a narrative where every meal, every bite, becomes a pivotal scene in the grand theater of your mental health.

Envision a journey where your plate transforms into a palette, painting not just sustenance but empowerment, not just nutrition but the rekindling of your inner flame. This isn't just a book—it's a symphony of science, mindfulness, culinary artistry, and self-discovery, woven together to orchestrate a transformative experience.

Join us as we embark on a 6-week expedition, a voyage that defies the conventions of typical wellness literature. Venture into the heart of nutritional psychiatry, as we delve into the fascinating tapestry that connects diet and mental well-being. From unraveling the mysteries of neurogenesis and forging a harmonious bond between gut and brain, to crafting plates that elevate your mood and nurturing a mindset of resilience, each chapter unfurls a treasure trove of knowledge and empowerment.

But this is not a solitary journey. "Nourishing the Mind" is not just a book; it's your trusted companion, your guide through the labyrinth of mental wellness. With every page you turn, you'll discover recipes that tantalize your taste buds while infusing your soul with the nutrients of self-care and growth—culinary therapy at its most potent.

In the chapters that await, you'll be transported through a tapestry of wisdom, a dance of empowerment, and a mosaic of transformation. You'll be privy to the alchemy of mindful eating, the exhilaration of movement, and the embrace of a nourished mindset. From the foundations of nutritional science to the intricacies of emotional healing, each piece of this mosaic contributes to a narrative of holistic well-being.

So, with anticipation in your heart and curiosity as your guide, let us set forth on this 6-week sojourn—a journey to nourish not only our bodies but also our minds. In your hands, you hold not just a book, but a key—an instrument of empowerment that opens the door to a world of possibility. The baton of the conductor is in your grasp, and the symphony of well-being is poised to begin. As the pages of "Nourishing the Mind" unfold, allow them to lead you towards a crescendo of strength, joy, and triumph over the shadows of depression and anxiety.

Chapter 1: The Science of Nutritional Psychiatry - Unveiling the Connection between Diet and Mental Health

In a world increasingly focused on quick fixes and pharmaceutical interventions for mental health issues, a burgeoning field of research known as nutritional psychiatry is shedding light on the profound impact that diet can have on mental well-being. This chapter serves as a gateway into the captivating realm of nutritional psychiatry, unraveling the intricate link between what we eat and how we feel.

The Mind-Gut Connection: A Prelude to Nutritional Psychiatry

In the intricate landscape of human health, the interplay between the mind and the gut has emerged as a captivating and pivotal area of exploration. This intricate relationship, often referred to as the "mind-gut connection" or the "gut-brain axis," lays the foundation for a profound understanding of the impact of diet on mental well-being. This phenomenon not only challenges the traditional boundaries of medical research but also provides a compelling prelude to the fascinating field of nutritional psychiatry.

At the heart of this connection lies an intricate network of communication pathways that facilitate a constant dialogue between the brain and the gut. The relationship is far from unidirectional; rather, it is a dynamic interplay that involves neural, hormonal, and immune mechanisms. This intricate system allows the gut to send signals to the brain, and vice versa, influencing a range of physiological and psychological processes.

Neural Communication: The Vagus Nerve's Role
One of the key conduits of communication between the mind and the gut is the vagus nerve—a remarkable neural highway that connects the brain to various organs, including the digestive system. This nerve serves as a biological telephone line, relaying messages in both directions. For instance, the gut sends signals to the brain about its state, including hunger, fullness, and discomfort. In return, the brain can transmit instructions that impact digestion, such as the release of digestive enzymes.

Hormonal Harmony: The Role of Gut Peptides
Hormones secreted by the gut, known as gut peptides, play a pivotal role in regulating appetite, mood, and even stress responses. These peptides send signals to the brain, influencing feelings of satiety and hunger. Moreover, certain gut peptides have been shown to impact mood and emotions. For instance, ghrelin, often referred to as the "hunger hormone," can influence mood regulation, indicating a direct link between the gut's hormonal signals and emotional well-being.

Microbial Mediators: The Gut Microbiome's Influence
The mind-gut connection extends even further to the microbial inhabitants of the digestive tract—the gut microbiome. This complex ecosystem of microorganisms not only aids in digestion but also plays a crucial role in shaping the brain-gut axis. The microbiome produces various metabolites and neurotransmitters that can influence mood and behavior. For example, the production of serotonin, often referred to as the "feel-good" neurotransmitter, is influenced by certain gut bacteria. This highlights the intricate ways in which the microbiome can impact mental health.

Emotions, Stress, and the Enteric Nervous System
Delving deeper into the mind-gut connection, researchers have uncovered the existence of an extensive network of neurons within the gut itself, known as the enteric nervous system (ENS). The ENS is often referred to as the "second brain" due to its ability to operate independently and communicate with the central nervous system. This system plays a significant role in regulating digestive processes but also has a direct impact on emotions and stress responses. This explains why emotional experiences can often manifest as physical sensations in the gut, and why stress can influence digestive discomfort.

The Bidirectional Link: Implications for Mental Health
The revelation of the mind-gut connection holds profound implications for mental health. It suggests that the health of the gut can influence mood, emotions, and cognitive

function, while mental states can in turn impact digestion and gut function. This bidirectional relationship is particularly relevant in understanding conditions such as irritable bowel syndrome (IBS), where emotional stress can exacerbate digestive symptoms, and conversely, digestive discomfort can trigger emotional distress.

In the context of nutritional psychiatry, the mind-gut connection underscores the need for a holistic approach to mental well-being—one that recognizes the intricate interplay between dietary choices, gut health, and emotional states. As we journey through the chapters of this book, we will uncover the scientific foundations that support the notion that nourishing the gut can also nourish the mind, ultimately offering a pathway to enhanced mental wellness.

Nutrients as Mood Modulators: A Journey through Biochemistry

In the intricate symphony of human physiology, the role of nutrients extends far beyond their fundamental function as fuel for the body. Emerging research has unveiled a captivating dimension of their influence on mental well-being—a dimension that delves deep into the realm of biochemistry. As we embark on this journey through the biochemical intricacies, we uncover how nutrients serve as potent mood modulators, shaping the delicate balance of neurotransmitters and emotions in ways that are both profound and transformative.

The Neurotransmitter Orchestra
At the heart of this biochemical narrative lie neurotransmitters—chemical messengers that facilitate communication between nerve cells, or neurons, within the brain. These molecules orchestrate a symphony of emotions, influencing everything from happiness and motivation to stress and anxiety. The journey into mood modulation begins with a closer look at some of the key players: serotonin, dopamine, and norepinephrine.

Serotonin: The Serene Regulator
Serotonin, often hailed as the "feel-good" neurotransmitter, is a cornerstone in the realm of mood regulation. It plays a pivotal role in modulating mood, anxiety, and even sleep. The raw material for serotonin synthesis is the amino acid tryptophan, which is obtained through diet. Understanding this connection sheds light on how dietary choices directly impact serotonin levels and subsequently influence emotional well-being.

Dopamine: The Motivation Molecule
Dopamine, another crucial neurotransmitter, is often associated with motivation, reward, and pleasure. This chemical messenger is synthesized from the amino acid tyrosine, which also finds its origins in dietary sources. The journey of tyrosine from plate to brain highlights the intricate interplay between dietary intake and emotional experiences. Low levels of dopamine have been linked to

conditions such as depression, further emphasizing the role of nutrients in mental health.

Norepinephrine: The Stress Responder

Norepinephrine, while playing a role in mood regulation, primarily acts as a stress hormone that readies the body for action. It is synthesized from dopamine and is crucial for the body's "fight or flight" response. The delicate balance between norepinephrine and other neurotransmitters contributes to emotional stability. Nutrients like vitamin C, found abundantly in fruits and vegetables, are known to support the production and regulation of norepinephrine.

Vitamins, Minerals, and Mood

Venturing further into the biochemical tapestry, we encounter vitamins and minerals as essential players in the mood modulation process. B vitamins, for instance, are critical co-factors in neurotransmitter synthesis. Vitamin B6, found in foods like bananas and poultry, aids in the conversion of tryptophan into serotonin. Folate, another B vitamin abundant in leafy greens, plays a role in neurotransmitter synthesis and has been linked to depression risk.

Omega-3 Fatty Acids: Nourishing the Brain

Omega-3 fatty acids, primarily sourced from fatty fish, walnuts, and flaxseeds, offer an intriguing connection between dietary choices and mental well-being. These fatty acids are structural components of brain cell membranes and play a role in regulating inflammation. Emerging research suggests that omega-3s may enhance serotonin and dopamine transmission, offering a potential explanation for their mood-boosting effects.

Antioxidants: Shields Against Oxidative Stress

The journey through mood-modulating nutrients would be incomplete without a mention of antioxidants. These compounds, abundant in colorful fruits and vegetables, play a pivotal role in combating oxidative stress—an imbalance linked to mood disorders. Antioxidants protect neurotransmitters from oxidative damage, thereby contributing to neurotransmitter balance and emotional stability.

Closing the Loop: The Nutrient-Emotion Nexus

As we conclude our exploration of nutrients as mood modulators, we recognize the intricate web of biochemical interactions that underpin emotional well-being. The journey through neurotransmitters, vitamins, minerals, and fatty acids reaffirms the notion that diet isn't just a source of energy; it's a blueprint for mental health. The choices we make at the dinner table influence the delicate balance of neurotransmitters that shape our emotions, offering a profound opportunity for individuals to actively contribute to their own emotional well-being.

Inflammation: The Silent Culprit

Building on the biochemical foundation, the chapter delves into the role of inflammation in mental health. Chronic inflammation, often triggered by poor dietary choices and lifestyle factors, is explored as a contributing factor to conditions like depression and anxiety. Readers are introduced to the concept of "neuroinflammation" and how it disrupts neural circuits, potentially leading to mood disorders.

The Mediterranean Diet: A Beacon of Hope
A significant portion of the chapter is dedicated to the Mediterranean diet—a dietary pattern that has garnered attention for its potential to promote mental well-being. The components of this diet, rich in fruits, vegetables, whole grains, lean proteins, and healthy fats, are dissected to reveal their collective impact on brain health. Scientific studies that showcase the Mediterranean diet's association with reduced risk of depression and cognitive decline are discussed, solidifying its role as a model for nutritional psychiatry.

The Microbiome's Influence: A Hidden Player in Mental Health
Shifting the focus to the gut microbiome, the chapter explores how the trillions of microorganisms residing in the digestive tract influence mental health. The role of gut microbiota in producing neurotransmitters, modulating inflammation, and communicating with the brain is explained. The chapter also touches on the potential of

prebiotics and probiotics to positively impact mental health by nurturing a balanced gut microbiome.

Beyond the Plate: Lifestyle Factors
While diet is central to nutritional psychiatry, the chapter also acknowledges the importance of lifestyle factors in the pursuit of mental well-being. It discusses the interplay between sleep, physical activity, stress management, and dietary choices. Readers gain insights into how these elements collectively contribute to mental health and are empowered to adopt a holistic approach.

Emerging Research and the Path Forward
Concluding the chapter is a glimpse into the exciting advancements in nutritional psychiatry research. Readers learn about ongoing studies that are unraveling new dimensions of the diet-mental health connection, including the potential of personalized nutrition in mental health interventions. The chapter also lays the groundwork for the chapters that follow, seamlessly setting the stage for a deeper exploration of nutrients, gut-brain harmony, and practical strategies.

Chapter 2: The Nutrient Arsenal for Brain Health - Exploring Twelve Essential Nutrients to Boost Cognitive Function

In the quest for optimal mental well-being, the role of nutrition transcends mere sustenance. Our dietary choices wield a profound impact on cognitive function, mood regulation, and overall brain health. This chapter delves into the intricate interplay between nutrients and the brain, unveiling a nutrient arsenal that has the potential to enhance cognitive prowess, elevate mood, and fortify mental resilience.

The Cognitive Canvas: A Nutrient-Rich Landscape

Imagine the brain as a canvas awaiting the strokes of nutrient-inspired brilliance. This chapter unfurls a palette of twelve essential nutrients that possess the power to influence neurochemistry, support neuronal growth, and protect brain cells from oxidative stress. As we journey through this nutrient-rich landscape, the intricate brushstrokes of biochemistry come to life, illuminating the potential of each nutrient to contribute to cognitive vibrancy.

Omega-3 Fatty Acids: Brain's Elixir of Fluidity

The chapter commences with a focus on omega-3 fatty acids, the cornerstone of brain health. Found abundantly in fatty fish like salmon and walnuts, these fats serve as structural components of brain cell membranes, enhancing their fluidity and communication efficiency. Omega-3s, particularly docosahexaenoic acid (DHA), play a critical role in neurogenesis—the birth of new brain cells—and are linked to improved cognitive function and reduced risk of cognitive decline.

B Vitamins: Sparking Cognitive Vitality

Venturing further into the nutrient realm, we encounter B vitamins as key players in cognitive vitality. B vitamins, including B6, B9 (folate), and B12, play a crucial role in neurotransmitter synthesis, influencing mood regulation and cognitive function. Folate, for instance, is involved in homocysteine metabolism; elevated homocysteine levels are associated with cognitive decline and an increased risk of dementia. The chapter illuminates dietary sources such as leafy greens, legumes, and fortified foods.

Vitamin D: Illuminating Cognitive Resilience

Vitamin D, often referred to as the "sunshine vitamin," transcends its role in bone health to influence cognitive resilience. Emerging research suggests a link between vitamin D deficiency and cognitive impairment, particularly in older adults. The chapter underscores the importance of safe sun exposure and dietary sources like fatty fish and fortified dairy products in maintaining optimal vitamin D levels.

Antioxidants: Shields Against Cognitive Decline

In the intricate balance between health and illness, the concept of oxidative stress emerges as a pivotal player, particularly when it comes to cognitive well-being. Oxidative stress, a state characterized by an imbalance between free radicals and the body's antioxidant defenses, is closely linked to cognitive decline and neurodegenerative diseases. This chapter dives deep into the world of antioxidants, unveiling their role as formidable shields against cognitive decline, and highlights the dietary sources and mechanisms through which they safeguard the brain.

Understanding Oxidative Stress: A Catalyst for Cognitive Decline

Before delving into the protective embrace of antioxidants, it's crucial to understand the concept of oxidative stress. Oxidative stress occurs when there's an excess of free radicals—unstable molecules that can damage cells—compared to the body's ability to neutralize them. This damage, known as oxidative damage, can occur in any part of the body, including the brain. It is a common feature of aging and is implicated in neurodegenerative conditions like Alzheimer's and Parkinson's disease.

Enter Antioxidants: Nature's Defenders

Antioxidants, as their name suggests, are compounds that counteract the damaging effects of oxidative stress. They neutralize free radicals by donating electrons, effectively preventing these radicals from causing cellular damage. The body produces its own antioxidants, but external sources—primarily derived from a diet rich in fruits, vegetables, nuts, and seeds—significantly contribute to bolstering the body's defense against oxidative stress.

Vitamin C: The Cellular Protector

Among the antioxidants, vitamin C emerges as a cellular protector of paramount significance. Found abundantly in citrus fruits, strawberries, bell peppers, and broccoli, vitamin C scavenges free radicals and regenerates other antioxidants like vitamin E. Its water-soluble nature allows it to roam freely within cells and body fluids, making it readily available to combat oxidative stress at various levels.

Vitamin E: The Lipid Guardian

Vitamin E takes on a distinct role as the lipid guardian, protecting cell membranes, including those of brain cells, from oxidative damage. It is a fat-soluble antioxidant found in nuts, seeds, vegetable oils, and leafy greens. By residing in cell membranes, vitamin E prevents the oxidation of lipids, which can result in cellular dysfunction and contribute to cognitive decline.

Polyphenols: Nature's Elixir of Protection

Polyphenols, a diverse group of plant compounds, encapsulate the protective potential of nature itself. Resveratrol, found in grapes and red wine, and quercetin, abundant in apples and onions, are just a glimpse of the rich tapestry of polyphenols. These compounds exhibit antioxidant and anti-inflammatory properties that extend to the brain. Their ability to cross the blood-brain barrier positions them as guardians of cognitive health.

The Brain's Antioxidant Army

Within the brain, a network of endogenous antioxidants stands guard against oxidative stress. Glutathione, a master antioxidant synthesized within cells, plays a crucial role in maintaining cellular health. N-acetylcysteine (NAC), a precursor to glutathione, serves as a potent supplement that boosts the brain's antioxidant defenses. Coenzyme Q10, explored earlier, also contributes to mitochondrial health and serves as an antioxidant within cells.

Dietary Strategies for Cognitive Protection

The chapter transitions from understanding the role of antioxidants to practical dietary strategies that promote cognitive protection. Incorporating a rainbow of fruits and vegetables ensures a diverse intake of antioxidants. Berries, rich in anthocyanins, and dark leafy greens, teeming with lutein and zeaxanthin, stand out as brain-boosting choices. Additionally, nuts, seeds, and whole grains provide vitamin E and selenium, reinforcing cognitive resilience.

Beyond Diet: Lifestyle Factors and Antioxidants

Antioxidant protection transcends diet alone. Lifestyle factors such as regular physical activity, stress management, and sufficient sleep contribute to the body's ability to combat oxidative stress. Adequate sleep, for instance, allows the brain to engage in cellular repair and detoxification processes that are vital for maintaining cognitive health.

Antioxidants and Cognitive Longevity
The chapter concludes by acknowledging the profound implications of antioxidants for cognitive longevity. By safeguarding brain cells from oxidative damage, antioxidants offer a means to not only preserve cognitive function as we age but also potentially delay the onset of neurodegenerative diseases. Their role in promoting overall brain health underscores the significance of adopting antioxidant-rich dietary patterns.

In the unfolding journey of nutritional psychiatry, antioxidants emerge as key protagonists in the narrative of cognitive wellness. Their ability to counteract the effects of oxidative stress serves as a beacon of hope for individuals seeking to maintain cognitive acuity and protect themselves against the shadows of cognitive decline. Through mindful dietary choices and lifestyle modifications, we embrace the potent potential of antioxidants to weave a tapestry of cognitive resilience and vitality.

Iron and Cognitive Vitality
Iron, a mineral often associated with physical vitality, also plays a crucial role in cognitive function. Iron is a key component of hemoglobin, the molecule that transports oxygen to brain cells. Insufficient iron levels can lead to anemia, resulting in cognitive impairment and reduced attention span. The chapter emphasizes the significance of dietary iron sources, such as lean meats, beans, and fortified cereals, in supporting cognitive vitality.

Zinc: Nurturing Neuronal Communication

Zinc, a trace mineral, contributes to cognitive function by supporting neuronal communication. It is involved in the synthesis of neurotransmitters and the maintenance of synaptic plasticity—the brain's ability to adapt and learn. Zinc's role in brain health is particularly relevant during periods of rapid growth and development, such as infancy and adolescence. Dietary sources, including seafood, poultry, and legumes, are explored in the chapter.

Magnesium: Calming the Cognitive Canvas

Magnesium, often associated with muscle relaxation, extends its influence on cognitive well-being. This mineral contributes to the regulation of neurotransmitters, including GABA, which plays a role in reducing anxiety and promoting relaxation. The chapter highlights how magnesium's role in stress reduction contributes to cognitive tranquility. Dietary sources, such as nuts, seeds, and leafy greens, are illuminated.

Choline: A Brain-Building Nutrient

Choline, a lesser-known nutrient, takes center stage in the chapter as a vital component of cell membranes and neurotransmitter synthesis. Choline's role in brain development and cognitive function is particularly crucial during fetal and early childhood stages. The chapter delves into dietary sources like eggs, liver, and soybeans that provide this brain-building nutrient.

Lutein and Zeaxanthin: Visionaries of Cognitive Health
The nutrient journey takes a turn towards the realm of vision as lutein and zeaxanthin emerge as visionaries of cognitive health. These carotenoids, predominantly found in leafy greens, serve as antioxidants that protect the retina from oxidative stress. Their presence in the retina contributes to visual acuity, a dimension of cognitive function often overlooked.

Coenzyme Q10: Energizing Cognitive Function
Coenzyme Q10, often abbreviated as CoQ10, shines as a cellular energy enhancer. Found in cells' mitochondria, CoQ10 supports energy production and offers protection against oxidative stress. The chapter unveils how CoQ10's role in cellular energy translates to cognitive vitality, underscoring its potential benefits for mental clarity and focus.

Selenium: Cognitive Guardian Against Oxidative Stress
Selenium, a trace mineral, emerges as a cognitive guardian against oxidative stress. This mineral supports the activity of antioxidant enzymes that defend brain cells from oxidative damage. The chapter explores dietary sources like Brazil nuts, seafood, and whole grains that offer selenium's protective embrace.

The Nutrient Symphony: A Harmonious Brain
As the chapter draws to a close, the intricate nutrient symphony resonates with the potential to craft a harmonious

brain—a brain that is fortified against cognitive decline, endowed with clarity of thought, and resilient in the face of challenges. The nutrient arsenal showcased in this chapter offers individuals a toolkit to nourish their cognitive potential and elevate their mental acumen.

In the chapters ahead, we will continue to unravel the intricacies of nutritional psychiatry, exploring how these essential nutrients can be harnessed as tools for mental wellness. With every nutrient-rich bite, we embark on a journey towards not only nourishing the body but also nurturing the intricate tapestry of cognitive function and emotional balance.

Chapter 3: Cultivating Neurogenesis - How Diet and Lifestyle Support the Birth of New Brain Cells

In the intricate realm of the brain, a process of remarkable significance unfolds—a process known as neurogenesis. Neurogenesis, the birth of new brain cells or neurons, defies the traditional notion that the brain's structure remains static throughout adulthood. This chapter delves deep into the intricate interplay between diet, lifestyle choices, and the promotion of neurogenesis. As we journey through the landscape of brain plasticity, we uncover the potential to harness this process for enhanced cognitive function, emotional well-being, and mental resilience.

The Marvel of Neurogenesis: A Paradigm Shift
The concept of neurogenesis challenges historical assumptions about brain development. Traditionally, it was believed that the brain ceased producing new neurons after a certain age. However, groundbreaking research has revealed the presence of neurogenesis in specific regions of the brain, particularly the hippocampus—a region crucial for learning, memory, and emotional regulation. This paradigm shift paves the way for exploring how various factors, including diet and lifestyle, can impact this rejuvenating process.

Neurotrophic Factors: Nurturing the Birth of Neurons
In the intricate landscape of the brain, a symphony of molecular signals orchestrates a remarkable phenomenon—neurogenesis, the birth of new neurons. At the heart of this symphony are neurotrophic factors, a group of proteins that play a pivotal role in nurturing the growth, survival, and integration of newly formed neurons. The exploration of neurotrophic factors unveils the intricate mechanisms that underlie the process of neurogenesis and offers a deeper

understanding of how these factors can be harnessed to enhance cognitive function and emotional well-being.

The Neurotrophic Landscape: An Overview

Neurotrophic factors, often referred to as "brain fertilizers," are a family of molecules that exert their effects primarily on neurons. They interact with specific receptors on the surface of neurons, triggering a cascade of intracellular events that ultimately influence the growth, differentiation, and survival of these cells. The discovery of these factors has revolutionized our understanding of brain plasticity—the brain's ability to adapt and reorganize itself.

BDNF: Brain-Derived Neurotrophic Factor

Among the neurotrophic factors, one stands out as a superstar—Brain-Derived Neurotrophic Factor (BDNF). BDNF is often described as a "master regulator" of neurogenesis due to its multifaceted roles in supporting neuronal growth and plasticity. This remarkable molecule is crucial for the development, survival, and function of neurons in various regions of the brain, especially the hippocampus—an area linked to memory and emotional regulation.

BDNF's Role in Synaptic Plasticity

BDNF's influence extends beyond neurogenesis—it plays a pivotal role in synaptic plasticity, the brain's ability to strengthen or weaken connections between neurons. This process underlies learning, memory, and adaptation to new experiences. BDNF promotes the formation and maturation of synapses, facilitating efficient communication between neurons. This interplay between neurogenesis and synaptic plasticity underscores the brain's remarkable capacity for adaptation.

Exercise and BDNF: A Dynamic Partnership

Physical activity emerges as a potent catalyst for BDNF release. Exercise triggers the release of BDNF, creating an environment that is conducive to neurogenesis and synaptic plasticity. Aerobic exercise, in particular, has been shown to enhance BDNF levels in the brain. This explains why engaging in regular physical activity is often associated with improved cognitive function, memory retention, and overall brain health.

Nutrition's Role in BDNF Synthesis

The diet also plays a role in nurturing the production of BDNF. Certain nutrients, particularly omega-3 fatty acids, flavonoids, and antioxidants, have been linked to increased BDNF levels. Omega-3s, found in fatty fish and flaxseeds, contribute to the formation of cell membranes and support neuronal growth. Flavonoids, abundant in colorful fruits and vegetables, exhibit antioxidant and anti-inflammatory properties that bolster BDNF production.

Stress, Depression, and BDNF

The interplay between BDNF and mental health is intricate and profound. Chronic stress and conditions like depression have been associated with reduced BDNF levels. Stress hormones, such as cortisol, can hinder BDNF production, impacting both neurogenesis and synaptic plasticity. This connection underscores the importance of strategies that mitigate stress, such as mindfulness, meditation, and social support, in maintaining optimal BDNF levels.

Lifestyle Strategies for Enhancing BDNF

As we navigate the relationship between BDNF and well-being, a spectrum of lifestyle strategies comes into focus. Engaging in regular aerobic exercise emerges as a powerful tool for boosting BDNF levels, promoting neurogenesis, and supporting cognitive function. Adequate sleep, stress management, and cognitive stimulation through challenging activities also contribute to an environment conducive to BDNF synthesis.

The Potential of BDNF for Mental Wellness

The exploration of neurotrophic factors, particularly BDNF, illuminates a pathway towards enhanced mental wellness. By understanding how lifestyle factors influence BDNF production, individuals are empowered to make choices that foster cognitive vitality and emotional resilience. The dynamic relationship between BDNF, neurogenesis, and synaptic plasticity offers a glimpse into the brain's incredible capacity for growth and adaptation.

Physical Activity: A Catalyst for Neuronal Birth

In the intricate dance of health and well-being, the impact of physical activity on the human body extends far beyond mere muscular strength and cardiovascular endurance.

Delving into the realm of the brain, physical activity emerges as a remarkable catalyst for a process of immense significance—neurogenesis, the birth of new neurons. This chapter explores the profound relationship between physical activity and neuronal birth, shedding light on the intricate mechanisms through which exercise fosters cognitive vitality, emotional resilience, and overall brain health.

The Neurogenic Oasis: Exercise's Impact on the Brain
Imagine the brain as an oasis—a place where cognitive growth flourishes. Physical activity serves as a key to this oasis, triggering a series of molecular events that nourish the birth of new neurons. The process of neurogenesis primarily occurs in the hippocampus, a region closely associated with learning, memory, and emotional regulation. As we engage in physical activity, we activate a cascade of factors that create an environment conducive to neuronal growth.

BDNF: A Star in the Neurogenesis Story
At the heart of exercise's impact on neurogenesis stands Brain-Derived Neurotrophic Factor (BDNF), a protein that plays a starring role in nurturing neuronal birth. BDNF acts as a growth promoter, supporting the survival, differentiation, and integration of newly formed neurons. Exercise triggers the release of BDNF, creating a molecular milieu that encourages neurogenesis. This connection between physical activity and BDNF levels underscores the brain's remarkable adaptability in response to external stimuli.

Aerobic Exercise: A Neurogenic Elixir
Aerobic exercise emerges as a particularly potent elixir for promoting neurogenesis. Activities such as running, swimming, and cycling engage large muscle groups and elevate heart rate, leading to an increased release of BDNF. This surge in BDNF levels creates an environment that nurtures the growth of new neurons and enhances synaptic plasticity—the brain's ability to adapt and learn. The hippocampus, a region rich in BDNF receptors, becomes a prime beneficiary of this exercise-induced neurogenic boost.

The Benefits of Intensity and Duration
The impact of physical activity on neurogenesis is nuanced, with intensity and duration playing pivotal roles. Studies suggest that moderate-intensity aerobic exercise has a more pronounced effect on BDNF release and neurogenesis compared to low-intensity activities. Additionally, engaging in longer-duration exercise sessions has been linked to increased BDNF levels, further enhancing the brain's potential for neuronal birth.

Neurogenesis Beyond the Sweat: Mind-Body Connection
While aerobic exercise takes center stage in the neurogenesis narrative, other forms of physical activity also contribute to neuronal birth. Mind-body practices, such as yoga and tai chi, offer a unique dimension to the relationship between movement and brain health. These

practices blend physical movement with mindfulness, fostering an environment that supports both neurogenesis and stress reduction—a holistic approach to brain wellness.

Age, Plasticity, and Exercise

The interplay between age and exercise in the realm of neurogenesis is both intriguing and encouraging. While the rate of neurogenesis may decline with age, exercise remains a potent tool for preserving cognitive function. Physical activity has been shown to counteract age-related decline in BDNF levels and promote neuronal birth even in older adults. This connection highlights the brain's capacity for plasticity—a quality that endorses lifelong opportunities for cognitive enhancement.

Creating a Neurogenic Lifestyle

As we navigate the intersection of physical activity and neurogenesis, the concept of creating a neurogenic lifestyle comes into focus. Regular exercise, whether in the form of brisk walks, jogging, dance, or any activity that elevates heart rate, contributes to the nurturing of neuronal birth. By incorporating physical activity into daily routines, individuals can actively engage in practices that support cognitive vitality and emotional well-being.

Diet's Impact on Neurogenesis: Nutrient Allies

As we delve deeper into the neurogenesis narrative, diet emerges as a powerful ally in supporting neuronal birth. Nutrients like omega-3 fatty acids, flavonoids, and antioxidants play pivotal roles. Omega-3s, abundant in fatty fish and flaxseeds, have been shown to enhance neurogenesis and cognitive function. Flavonoids, found in colorful fruits and vegetables, exhibit neuroprotective effects and support the growth of new neurons.

Caloric Restriction: A Double-Edged Sword

Caloric restriction, a dietary strategy involving reduced calorie intake without malnutrition, presents a double-edged sword in the context of neurogenesis. On one hand, it has been linked to increased BDNF levels and enhanced neurogenesis. On the other hand, extreme caloric restriction can lead to nutrient deficiencies, which may hinder the neurogenesis process. The chapter navigates this delicate balance and highlights the importance of a balanced approach.

Intermittent Fasting and Neuronal Renewal

Intermittent fasting, an eating pattern that alternates between periods of eating and fasting, also emerges as a player in the neurogenesis narrative. This dietary strategy triggers the release of BDNF and enhances the brain's resilience to stress. The chapter explores the potential benefits of intermittent fasting on neuronal renewal and its broader implications for cognitive health.

Social Interaction and Mental Stimulation

Beyond diet, social interaction and mental stimulation contribute to the nurturing of neurogenesis. Engaging in meaningful social activities and challenging cognitive tasks has been shown to enhance BDNF levels and promote the birth of new neurons. These factors underscore the holistic approach required for fostering neurogenesis and optimizing cognitive function.

Stress and Neurogenesis: A Delicate Balance

Stress, often regarded as a disruptor of well-being, also intertwines with the neurogenesis narrative. Acute stress can trigger the release of hormones that impact neurogenesis, while chronic stress can hinder this process. The chapter emphasizes the importance of stress management techniques, such as mindfulness and meditation, in maintaining a conducive environment for neuronal birth.

Sleep: A Pillar of Neurogenesis

Sleep, a cornerstone of health, emerges as a pillar of neurogenesis. During sleep, the brain undergoes processes that promote cellular repair and detoxification, supporting the growth of new neurons. The chapter explores the relationship between sleep quality and neurogenesis, underscoring the significance of prioritizing restful sleep for cognitive vitality.

Environmental Enrichment: A Vibrant Ecosystem for the Brain

Environmental enrichment, encompassing novel experiences, sensory stimulation, and exposure to complex environments, acts as a vibrant ecosystem for the brain. This enriched environment has been shown to enhance neurogenesis and boost cognitive function. The chapter unveils the potential of cultivating an environment that nourishes both the mind and the brain.

Neurogenesis: A Lifelong Opportunity for Growth

As the chapter reaches its crescendo, it paints a portrait of neurogenesis as a lifelong opportunity for growth and renewal. The brain's ability to generate new neurons presents a canvas for individuals to actively engage in practices that promote cognitive vitality and emotional resilience. The potential for enhancing neurogenesis through diet, physical activity, social engagement, stress management, and sleep emerges as a profound pathway to optimizing brain health.

In the chapters ahead, we continue to unravel the intricate relationship between lifestyle choices, nutrition, and mental well-being. As we delve into the strategies and practices that support neurogenesis, we embrace the dynamic journey of neuronal birth—a journey that affirms the brain's remarkable capacity for growth, adaptation, and transformation.

Chapter 4: Gut-Brain Harmony - Strategies to Foster a Healthy Gut Microbiome for Improved Mental Well-being

The intricate connection between the gut and the brain forms the foundation of a rapidly evolving field known as the gut-brain axis. This chapter delves deep into the fascinating interplay between the gut microbiome—the trillions of microorganisms residing in our digestive tract—and its profound impact on mental well-being. As we explore the intricate mechanisms that link the gut and the brain, we uncover strategies to cultivate a healthy gut microbiome as a means to support cognitive function, emotional resilience, and overall mental health.

The Gut-Brain Axis: A Bi-Directional Communication Highway

Imagine a communication highway that spans from your gut to your brain—a highway through which information flows bidirectionally, influencing both physical and mental well-being. This is the gut-brain axis, a complex network of biochemical signals that connects the gut microbiome with brain function. This chapter unravels the intricate mechanisms of this axis and its implications for mental health.

The Gut Microbiome: A Microscopic Ecosystem
At the heart of the gut-brain axis lies the gut microbiome, a diverse community of bacteria, viruses, fungi, and other microorganisms that inhabit the digestive tract. This ecosystem not only aids in digestion but also plays a crucial role in immune function, nutrient absorption, and the synthesis of important molecules. Recent research has unveiled its role in influencing brain function and mental health.

Microbiota-Gut-Brain Communication: The Molecular Language
The gut microbiome communicates with the brain through a molecular language that involves hormones, neurotransmitters, and immune molecules. For example, the gut microbiota can produce neurotransmitters like serotonin and dopamine, which play key roles in mood regulation. The microbiome also interacts with the immune system, producing molecules that can affect brain function and mental well-being.

The Brain's Microbial Orchestra: Influences on Mood and Behavior

The gut microbiome's influence on mood and behavior is a revelation that has transformed our understanding of mental health. Research has shown that alterations in the gut microbiome composition are associated with conditions like anxiety, depression, and even neurodevelopmental disorders. The chapter delves into the intricate web of interactions that impact mood and behavior through the gut-brain axis.

The Second Brain: The Enteric Nervous System

Deep within the confines of the human body lies a hidden marvel—an intricate network of nerves and neurons known as the enteric nervous system (ENS). Often referred to as the "second brain," the ENS is a captivating revelation that highlights the complexity of the gut-brain axis—a bidirectional communication system that connects the gut and the central nervous system. This chapter delves into the enigmatic realm of the enteric nervous system, unraveling its significance, functions, and the profound implications it holds for mental well-being.

The Enteric Nervous System Unveiled

The enteric nervous system is a branch of the autonomic nervous system that operates independently, yet in close communication with, the central nervous system. It consists of an intricate network of neurons that extend from the esophagus to the rectum, orchestrating the complex processes of digestion, absorption, and gut motility. With over 100 million neurons—more than the spinal cord—the ENS forms an intricate web that oversees the gut's functional intricacies.

A Mind of Its Own: The ENS's Autonomy

One of the most fascinating aspects of the enteric nervous system is its autonomy. The ENS can regulate the processes of digestion and absorption without direct input from the brain. It operates through reflexes that initiate in response to stimuli within the gut, allowing it to function independently even in the absence of input from the central nervous system. This autonomy grants the ENS its moniker—the "second brain."

Neurotransmitters and the ENS-Brain Dialogue

Communication between the enteric nervous system and the central nervous system is facilitated by an array of neurotransmitters and chemical messengers. These molecules bridge the gap between the gut and the brain, allowing them to influence each other's function. For example, neurotransmitters like serotonin, often associated with mood regulation, are produced in large quantities within the gut and play a role in both gut motility and mood.

Gut-Brain Interactions: The ENS's Influence on Mood

Research has shown that the enteric nervous system's influence extends beyond digestion and gut function—it also impacts mood and emotional states. The gut-brain axis allows bidirectional communication between the gut and the brain, enabling the ENS to influence mood regulation and emotional responses. This connection is a key factor in understanding how gut health can impact mental well being.

Stress and the ENS: A Complex Relationship

Stress, a significant influencer of both gut and brain function, plays a complex role in the enteric nervous system's dynamics. Stress can impact gut motility, alter gut permeability, and contribute to conditions like irritable bowel syndrome (IBS). Conversely, gut distress caused by factors like dysbiosis can trigger stress responses in the central nervous system, creating a feedback loop that affects both systems.

Microbiome and the ENS: A Synergistic Alliance

The gut microbiome, the community of microorganisms residing in the digestive tract, plays an integral role in shaping the enteric nervous system's function. Microbes within the gut contribute to the production of neurotransmitters, modulating the ENS's influence on mood and behavior. Conversely, the ENS regulates gut motility, creating an environment that impacts the composition and diversity of the gut microbiome.

The ENS and Mental Health Disorders

Understanding the connection between the enteric nervous system and mental health disorders offers new avenues for therapeutic interventions. Conditions like irritable bowel syndrome (IBS), which is characterized by gastrointestinal symptoms and often co-occurs with mood disorders like anxiety and depression, highlight the intricate interplay between the gut and the brain. By addressing the gut-brain axis, novel treatments may emerge.

Nurturing the Second Brain: A Holistic Approach
Cultivating a healthy enteric nervous system involves a holistic approach that encompasses diet, stress management, and lifestyle choices. Consuming a diet rich in fiber and fermented foods supports gut health and the growth of beneficial gut bacteria. Stress-reduction techniques, such as mindfulness and meditation, can also positively impact the ENS by modulating stress-related responses.

Dysbiosis and Mental Health: A Troubled Harmony
Dysbiosis, an imbalance in the gut microbiome composition, emerges as a potential disruptor of gut-brain harmony. This imbalance can result from factors like poor diet, stress, antibiotics, and more. Dysbiosis is linked to inflammation, which can impact brain function and contribute to mood disorders. The chapter highlights the intricate relationship between gut health and mental well-being.

Probiotics and Prebiotics: Nurturing the Gut Microbiome

The concept of modulating the gut microbiome to enhance mental health is supported by the use of probiotics and prebiotics. Probiotics are live microorganisms that confer health benefits when consumed, while prebiotics are dietary fibers that nourish beneficial gut bacteria. Research suggests that specific strains of probiotics can have positive effects on mood and anxiety.

Diet's Impact on the Gut-Brain Axis: A Holistic Approach

The Diet emerges as a key player in nurturing a healthy gut microbiome and supporting mental well-being. A diet rich in fiber, whole foods, and fermented foods provides the nutrients necessary for the growth of beneficial gut bacteria. On the other hand, a diet high in refined sugars and processed foods can lead to dysbiosis and inflammation, potentially affecting brain health.

Stress, Gut Permeability, and Inflammation

Stress, a ubiquitous aspect of modern life, exerts its influence on the gut-brain axis. Chronic stress can lead to increased gut permeability, often referred to as "leaky gut." This condition allows harmful substances to enter the bloodstream, triggering an immune response and inflammation. In turn, inflammation can impact brain function and contribute to mental health issues.

Mind-Gut Interventions: Stress Management and Mindfulness

The chapter explores mind-gut interventions that foster a harmonious relationship between stress management, mindfulness, and gut health. Techniques like mindfulness meditation and deep breathing have been shown to reduce stress and inflammation, positively influencing the gut microbiome and subsequently supporting mental well-being.

Personalizing Gut Health for Mental Wellness

As research continues to uncover the intricate links between the gut microbiome and mental health, a personalized approach to gut health emerges as a promising avenue. The concept of "precision nutrition" takes into account an individual's unique gut microbiome composition and dietary preferences to develop strategies that support both gut health and mental well-being.

Embracing the Gut-Brain Connection for Mental Wellness

The chapter concludes by highlighting the transformative potential of embracing the gut-brain connection for mental wellness. By nurturing a healthy gut microbiome through dietary choices, stress management, and mindful interventions, individuals can actively engage in practices that promote cognitive function, emotional balance, and overall mental well-being.

In the unfolding journey of nutritional psychiatry, the gut-brain axis stands as a testament to the intricate interplay of body and mind. As we navigate the multifaceted relationship between the gut microbiome and mental health, we embark on a path that celebrates the potential of holistic well-being—one that honors the harmony between the gut and the brain.

Chapter 5: Crafting Your Mood-Boosting Plate - Curating a Diet to Alleviate Depression and Soothe Anxiety

The notion that "you are what you eat" has transcended its conventional wisdom and found resonance in the realm of mental health. The connection between diet and emotional well-being is increasingly recognized, emphasizing the power of nutrition to influence mood, alleviate depression, and soothe anxiety. This chapter embarks on a journey to explore the intricate relationship between diet and mental health, offering insights into the nutrients, dietary patterns, and mindful practices that can shape a mood-boosting plate.

The Nutritional Foundations of Mood Regulation

At the heart of crafting a mood-boosting plate lies an understanding of the nutrients that contribute to mood regulation. Nutrients are the building blocks that support neurotransmitter synthesis, hormonal balance, and cellular energy production—critical components of emotional equilibrium. Vitamins, minerals, and antioxidants collaborate in this intricate orchestra of biochemical processes that impact mental health.

Omega-3 Fatty Acids: The Brain's Allies

Omega-3 fatty acids, particularly eicosapentaenoic acid (EPA) and docosahexaenoic acid (DHA), are celebrated for their role in supporting brain health and emotional well-being. These essential fatty acids, abundantly found in fatty fish like salmon, flaxseeds, and walnuts, are integral to maintaining the fluidity of cell membranes. This fluidity influences the activity of neurotransmitter receptors, ensuring optimal neuronal communication.

The Mood-Boosting Mechanisms of Omega-3s

The influence of omega-3s on mood is underpinned by their impact on neurotransmitters. EPA, in particular, is associated with reducing inflammation, a process often linked to mood disorders. Additionally, omega-3s play a role in the production of serotonin and dopamine—neurotransmitters that regulate mood and pleasure. Research suggests that adequate omega-3 intake may alleviate symptoms of depression and anxiety, offering a natural approach to mental well-being.

B Vitamins: The Mood Enhancers

B vitamins, a family of water-soluble vitamins, each carry unique contributions to mood health. Folate (B9) is essential for the synthesis of neurotransmitters like serotonin and dopamine, which play pivotal roles in regulating mood. Vitamin B12, on the other hand, supports the production of myelin—a protective sheath around nerve fibers. Inadequate intake of these vitamins has been linked to mood disorders.

Magnesium and Zinc: Minerals for Calmness

The minerals magnesium and zinc contribute to a sense of calmness and emotional stability. Magnesium is a cofactor in over 300 biochemical reactions, including those related to neurotransmitter synthesis and the regulation of stress hormones. Zinc participates in the conversion of tryptophan to serotonin, highlighting its role in mood regulation. Ensuring sufficient intake of these minerals supports emotional well-being.

Antioxidants: Cellular Protectors and Mood Elevators

Antioxidants, renowned for their role in neutralizing oxidative stress, extend their protective influence to the brain. Vitamins C and E, along with phytonutrients like flavonoids, exhibit antioxidant properties that shield brain cells from damage and inflammation. These compounds contribute to the synthesis of neurotransmitters that impact mood, further highlighting the importance of a diet rich in colorful fruits and vegetables.

The Mediterranean Diet: A Blueprint for Mood Health

The Mediterranean diet, revered for its health benefits, emerges as a dietary blueprint for promoting mood health.

This dietary pattern is characterized by an abundance of whole foods, including fruits, vegetables, whole grains, lean proteins, and healthy fats like olive oil and nuts. Research suggests that adhering to the Mediterranean diet is associated with a reduced risk of depression and anxiety.

Nutrients Beyond the Plate: The Gut-Brain Connection
The relationship between diet and mood extends beyond direct nutrient intake to encompass the gut-brain connection. The gut microbiome, a complex ecosystem of microorganisms residing in the digestive tract, plays a pivotal role in mood regulation. Beneficial gut bacteria contribute to the production of neurotransmitters like serotonin, influencing emotional well-being.

Inflammation and Mood: The Role of Diet
Chronic inflammation has been implicated in mood disorders such as depression. Diet plays a significant role in modulating inflammation levels within the body. Certain foods, such as those high in refined sugars and unhealthy fats, contribute to pro-inflammatory states, while a diet rich in whole foods, fruits, vegetables, and healthy fats can have anti-inflammatory effects. By curating an anti-inflammatory diet, individuals can potentially support their mood health.

Mindful Eating: Nurturing Emotional Resilience
The concept of mindful eating transcends the realm of nutrients to encompass the psychological aspects of food consumption. Mindful eating involves being fully present

during meals, savoring each bite, and paying attention to the sensory experiences of eating. This practice fosters a healthier relationship with food, enhances appreciation for nourishment, and can contribute to emotional resilience.

In the journey towards optimal mental well-being, the chapter on crafting a mood-boosting plate is a guide to transforming dietary choices into a form of self-care. By understanding the role of specific nutrients in neurotransmitter synthesis, hormonal balance, and cellular function, individuals gain insights into how their diet can shape their emotional state. This chapter not only provides knowledge but also empowers individuals to take an active role in their mental health journey.

A Holistic Approach to Nourishment
Crafting a mood-boosting plate is not a singular endeavor focused solely on isolated nutrients; it's a holistic approach to nourishment. The art of combining omega-3 fatty acids, B vitamins, magnesium, zinc, antioxidants, and other mood-supportive nutrients involves curating a diverse and balanced diet. This approach acknowledges the synergistic interactions between nutrients and their collective impact on emotional resilience.

The Mediterranean Diet as a Lifestyle Choice
The Mediterranean diet, in its embodiment of whole foods, healthy fats, and plant-based nutrition, transcends mere sustenance to become a lifestyle choice. Beyond its benefits

for mood health, it also contributes to heart health, longevity, and overall well-being. Embracing the principles of the Mediterranean diet reflects a commitment to a way of eating that harmonizes with the body's nutritional needs and supports mental health along the way.

Mindful Eating: The Gateway to Connection
Mindful eating is more than a dietary practice; it's a form of mindful living. Engaging in mindful eating fosters a deeper connection with the present moment, transforming meals into opportunities for self-awareness and nourishment. By savoring each bite, acknowledging the textures and flavors, and cultivating gratitude for the food on the plate, individuals cultivate a relationship with food that transcends mere nutrition.

Nutrition's Role in Preventative Mental Health
The chapter also raises the concept of nutrition as a preventative strategy for mental health disorders. While therapeutic interventions remain crucial, there is growing recognition of the potential for nutrition to act as a protective shield against the onset of mood disorders. By adopting a diet rich in mood-supportive nutrients and practicing mindful eating, individuals may reduce their risk of experiencing depression and anxiety.

Cultivating Resilience: A Nourishing Practice
The act of crafting a mood-boosting plate is an act of self-care and resilience. It involves making conscious choices that honor both physical and emotional well-being. This

practice encourages individuals to view food as a tool for nourishment, empowerment, and self-compassion. It challenges the notion of food as a mere source of calories and reframes it as a vehicle for nurturing vitality and vitality.

Adapting and Personalizing the Approach
Individuality remains central in the journey of crafting a mood-boosting plate. While general guidelines provide a foundation, each person's nutritional needs and preferences are unique. The chapter encourages individuals to listen to their bodies, pay attention to how different foods make them feel, and adapt their dietary choices accordingly. Personalization ensures that the approach to nutrition aligns with individual goals and well-being.

A Pathway to Wholeness
As the chapter draws to a close, it emphasizes the transformative potential of crafting a mood-boosting plate. The act of selecting and savoring foods becomes a form of self-expression, a way to honor one's health and happiness. By embracing the intricate relationship between diet and mood, individuals embark on a journey that embodies the essence of holistic well-being—a journey that nurtures not only the body but also the mind and spirit.

In the unfolding narrative of nutritional psychiatry, the chapter on crafting a mood-boosting plate stands as a testament to the profound impact of dietary choices on mental health. As individuals curate their plates with intention, they are engaging in an act of self-love—one that nourishes not only their bodies but also their emotional well-being. By embracing the connection between nutrition and mood, individuals pave a path toward a life enriched with vitality, emotional equilibrium, and the joy of nourishment.

Chapter 6: Beyond the Plate: Lifestyle Challenges - Identifying Modern Hurdles to Healthy Eating and Mental Wellness

As we navigate the journey towards mental well-being through nutritional psychiatry, it becomes clear that the path extends beyond the confines of the plate. The modern world presents a myriad of lifestyle challenges that can hinder our efforts to cultivate healthy eating habits and foster emotional equilibrium. This chapter delves into the intricate web of lifestyle challenges, exploring how factors such as time constraints, stress, convenience culture, and digital distractions can impact our relationship with food and mental wellness.

Time Scarcity and the "Busy" Culture

In the hustle and bustle of modern life, time often feels like a scarce resource. The demands of work, family, and social commitments can lead to rushed meals and inadequate attention to nutrition. This challenge intersects with mental wellness as hurried eating may disrupt the digestive process, impair nutrient absorption, and compromise mindful eating practices. Addressing time scarcity involves prioritizing self-care and finding strategies to integrate nourishing meals into a busy schedule.

Stress and Emotional Eating

In the fast-paced and demanding world of today, stress has become a ubiquitous companion. As we navigate the intricacies of work, relationships, and personal responsibilities, stress often weaves itself into the fabric of daily life. Yet, the relationship between stress and our dietary choices is a complex one, often resulting in a phenomenon known as emotional eating. This intricate connection between our emotions, stress, and eating habits sheds light on a behavior that can have significant implications for our mental and physical well-being.

Understanding Emotional Eating

Emotional eating refers to the act of consuming food in response to emotional triggers rather than physiological hunger. It's a coping mechanism that provides temporary comfort and relief from negative emotions such as stress, anxiety, sadness, or boredom. When faced with challenging emotions, individuals may turn to food as a source of solace, seeking a momentary distraction from their emotional discomfort.

The Neurobiology of Stress and Eating

The brain's response to stress involves a complex interplay of hormones, neurotransmitters, and neural circuits. When stress arises, the body releases cortisol—a hormone often referred to as the "stress hormone." Cortisol influences appetite regulation by stimulating the brain's reward centers and increasing cravings for high-calorie and palatable foods. This physiological response, coupled with the psychological comfort that food can provide, sets the stage for emotional eating.

Emotional Eating: The Temporary Escape

Emotional eating offers a brief escape from the intensity of negative emotions. The act of eating releases dopamine, a neurotransmitter associated with pleasure and reward, which can temporarily alleviate stress and anxiety. This instant gratification reinforces the association between emotional discomfort and the act of eating, creating a cycle that can be difficult to break.

The Pitfalls of Emotional Eating

While emotional eating may provide transient relief, it often comes with consequences. Consuming high-calorie, sugary, or salty comfort foods can lead to overeating and weight gain over time. Moreover, the relief obtained from emotional eating is short-lived, and the original emotions that triggered the behavior often resurface once the eating episode is over. This can lead to feelings of guilt, shame, and an increased cycle of emotional eating as individuals seek to escape those negative emotions once again.

Breaking the Cycle: Strategies for Managing Emotional Eating
Recognizing and managing emotional eating is a crucial step towards fostering a healthy relationship with food and emotional well-being. Several strategies can assist in breaking the cycle:

1. Emotional Awareness: Developing mindfulness around emotional triggers is essential. Recognizing when stress or other emotions are driving the urge to eat can help individuals pause and make conscious choices.

2. Healthy Coping Mechanisms: Identifying alternative ways to cope with stress is vital. Engaging in activities such as exercise, meditation, journaling, or connecting with loved ones can provide healthier outlets for managing emotions.

3. Mindful Eating: Practicing mindful eating involves being fully present during meals, savoring each bite, and paying attention to hunger and fullness cues. This practice can help individuals differentiate between true physiological hunger and emotional cravings.

4. Building Resilience: Developing emotional resilience through stress management techniques like deep breathing, progressive muscle relaxation, and cognitive reframing can reduce the frequency of emotional eating episodes.

5. Seeking Support: For those struggling with chronic stress or emotional eating, seeking professional help from therapists, counselors, or registered dietitians can provide tailored strategies and support.

Embracing Emotional Well-Being
Understanding the interplay between stress and emotional eating reveals the importance of addressing the root causes of our dietary choices. Emotional eating isn't merely about willpower; it's a response to complex emotional dynamics. By cultivating emotional awareness, learning healthier coping mechanisms, and fostering mindfulness, individuals can transform their relationship with food and their ability to manage stress. This shift not only supports mental well-being but also empowers individuals to embrace a more balanced and resilient approach to life's challenges.

The Convenience Culture and Processed Foods

The allure of convenience often leads individuals to rely on processed and fast foods, which are typically high in calories, sodium, and additives. These foods, while offering immediate gratification, can compromise overall health and mental wellness. The nutrient deficiencies associated with processed foods can impact brain function, mood regulation, and cognitive performance. Combating the convenience culture involves planning and preparing wholesome meals ahead of time, emphasizing whole foods that support mental health.

Digital Distractions and Mindful Eating

The digital age has introduced a new challenge to healthy eating: constant connectivity and digital distractions. Engaging with screens during meals can disrupt the practice of mindful eating—a technique that encourages being fully present and attuned to the sensory experience of eating. This detachment from the act of eating can lead to overconsumption and reduced satisfaction from meals. Cultivating mindful eating involves creating designated technology-free eating spaces and fostering a connection with food.

Social Pressures and Eating Habits

Social gatherings and cultural norms often revolve around food, and navigating these scenarios can be challenging for individuals striving to maintain a balanced diet and mental wellness. Social pressures to indulge in unhealthy foods or conform to others' eating habits can create feelings of conflict and guilt. Developing strategies to assertively communicate dietary choices, seeking supportive social circles, and practicing self-compassion are vital in overcoming these challenges.

Sleep Deprivation and Dietary Choices
The link between sleep and mental wellness is well-established. Sleep deprivation not only impairs cognitive function and mood regulation but also impacts dietary choices. Sleep-deprived individuals are more likely to crave high-calorie, sugary foods and experience reduced satiety. This cycle of poor sleep and suboptimal food choices can create a detrimental feedback loop that undermines both physical and mental health. Prioritizing adequate sleep hygiene and creating a sleep-supportive environment can break this cycle.

Self-Care Deficits and Burnout
The lack of self-care can contribute to burnout—an emotional, physical, and mental state characterized by exhaustion and reduced productivity. Burnout can lead to erratic eating patterns, reliance on convenience foods, and decreased engagement in mindful eating practices. Prioritizing self-care activities such as exercise, relaxation techniques, and hobbies not only supports mental wellness but also fosters a positive relationship with food and nourishment.

Cultivating Resilience Through Lifestyle Choices

As the chapter unfolds, it underscores the importance of recognizing and addressing these lifestyle challenges as integral components of the mental health journey. The interplay between nutrition, lifestyle, and mental wellness is complex and multifaceted. By acknowledging the impact of time constraints, stress, convenience culture, digital distractions, and social pressures, individuals can proactively seek solutions that foster resilience and promote holistic well-being.

Strategies for Lifestyle Integration

The chapter concludes by offering practical strategies to integrate mental wellness-focused choices into everyday life. From time management techniques and stress-reduction practices to mindful technology usage and assertive communication, these strategies empower individuals to navigate lifestyle challenges while staying committed to their mental health goals. The holistic approach advocated throughout the chapter emphasizes the harmonious interplay between dietary choices, lifestyle habits, and emotional well-being.

Navigating Lifestyle Challenges with Compassion

In the narrative of nutritional psychiatry, the chapter on lifestyle challenges reminds us that the journey toward mental well-being is a dynamic and evolving process. It's not about achieving perfection but rather about cultivating self-awareness, embracing challenges with compassion, and making intentional choices that align with our values and goals. By recognizing the complexities of modern life and adopting strategies that support mental wellness, individuals pave a path to resilience, balance, and a nourished mind and spirit.

PART 2: EMBARKING ON YOUR HEALING JOURNEY

Chapter 7: Becoming Your Own Nutritional Therapist - Empowering Yourself with Mindful Eating and Intuitive Nutrition

In the pursuit of optimal mental well-being, individuals are not merely passive recipients of advice; they possess the capacity to become their own agents of change. Chapter 7 embarks on a journey of self-empowerment, exploring the concepts of mindful eating and intuitive nutrition as tools for fostering a harmonious relationship with food, promoting emotional resilience, and nurturing a sense of well-being. This chapter empowers readers to embrace their innate wisdom and become their own nutritional therapists.

The Art of Mindful Eating

Mindful eating is an ancient practice that invites individuals to bring full awareness to the act of eating. It involves being present in the moment, savoring each bite, and paying attention to the sensory experiences of taste, smell, texture, and color. This deliberate engagement with food fosters a deep connection between mind and body, encouraging a more conscious and intentional approach to nourishment.

Principles of Mindful Eating

Mindful eating is guided by several principles that encourage a mindful and intentional relationship with food:

1. Eat with Awareness: Being fully present while eating, free from distractions, allows individuals to fully experience their meals and recognize cues of hunger and satiety.

2. Savor the Experience: Engaging the senses by appreciating the flavors, aromas, and textures of food enhances the enjoyment of eating and deepens the satisfaction derived from meals.

3. Listen to Your Body: Tuning into internal cues of hunger and fullness helps individuals recognize when to start and stop eating, promoting a balanced intake that aligns with the body's needs.

4. Non-Judgmental Attitude: Approaching eating with a non-judgmental mindset, free from guilt or criticism,

encourages self-compassion and a positive relationship with food.

Benefits of Mindful Eating
The practice of mindful eating extends its benefits beyond the realm of nutrition. Research suggests that mindful eating can:

1. Improve digestion and nutrient absorption by facilitating proper chewing and digestion.
2. Reduce overeating and weight gain by enhancing awareness of hunger and fullness cues.
3. Diminish emotional eating by fostering a deeper understanding of the emotional triggers for eating.
4. Enhance satisfaction and enjoyment of meals, leading to a greater sense of well-being.

Intuitive Nutrition: Embracing Inner Wisdom
Intuitive nutrition is rooted in the belief that individuals possess innate wisdom to make food choices that align with their bodies' needs. It encourages a departure from rigid diets and external rules, inviting individuals to trust their internal cues and preferences. Intuitive eaters make choices based on hunger, fullness, and the desire for nourishing foods that offer both physical and emotional satisfaction.

Principles of Intuitive Nutrition

Intuitive nutrition operates on a set of principles that guide individuals in making food choices that honor their bodies:

1. Reject Diet Mentality: Letting go of restrictive diets and embracing a compassionate approach to eating is foundational to intuitive nutrition.

2. Honor Hunger: Paying attention to biological hunger cues and responding with nourishing foods supports overall well-being.

3. Respect Fullness: Tuning into signals of fullness and stopping eating when satisfied promotes a balanced intake.

4. Make Peace with Food: Allowing all foods without judgment helps eliminate feelings of guilt or deprivation.

5. Discover Satisfaction: Seeking foods that bring both physical and emotional satisfaction contributes to a positive relationship with eating.

Benefits of Intuitive Nutrition
The practice of intuitive nutrition offers a host of benefits that extend beyond nutritional health:
1. Fostering body acceptance and self-esteem by promoting a positive body image.

2. Reduces the tendency to binge eat or feel out of control around food.
3. Supports emotional well-being by allowing for flexibility and spontaneity in food choices.
4. Enhances the enjoyment of meals, leading to a more joyful and balanced approach to eating.

Cultivating Mindful Eating and Intuitive Nutrition
The chapter emphasizes that mindful eating and intuitive nutrition are not one-size-fits-all practices. They involve a process of self-discovery and continuous learning. Cultivating these practices involves:

1. Self-Awareness: Reflecting on eating habits, emotional triggers, and attitudes toward food.
2. Mindful Practice: Integrating mindful eating into meals by slowing down, savoring each bite, and avoiding distractions.
3. Tuning In: Listening to internal hunger and fullness cues and trusting the body's wisdom.
4. Embracing Flexibility: Allowing for a variety of foods and making choices that honor both nutritional needs and preferences.

Empowering Self-Nutritional Therapy
The journey of self-nutritional therapy is a voyage of self-discovery, personal growth, and empowerment. It's a departure from external rules and restrictions, and an embrace of inner wisdom and intuition. By embracing mindful eating and intuitive nutrition, individuals embark on a path that not only nourishes their bodies but also

nurtures their mental well-being and fosters a positive relationship with food.

Mindful Eating as a Daily Practice

Incorporating mindful eating into daily life requires dedication and practice. The key lies in cultivating a sense of mindfulness that extends beyond mealtimes. Mindfulness involves being present in each moment, whether it's chopping vegetables, sipping tea, or enjoying a meal with loved ones. As individuals engage in these moments with full awareness, they create opportunities to deepen their connection with the nourishment they provide to their bodies and minds.

Listening to the Wisdom Within

Intuitive nutrition is an invitation to listen to the body's cues and trust its innate wisdom. This involves letting go of external rules and restrictions and tuning into the signals of hunger, fullness, and satisfaction. It requires embracing food as a source of pleasure, nourishment, and emotional well-being. By learning to distinguish between true physiological hunger and emotional cravings, individuals can make choices that honor their bodies' needs.

Unlearning Diet Culture and Embracing Body Positivity

Central to the practice of mindful eating and intuitive nutrition is unlearning the influence of diet culture. Society often promotes unrealistic ideals of body image and perpetuates the idea that certain foods are "good" while others are "bad." This dichotomy can lead to feelings of guilt and shame around eating. Embracing body positivity and practicing self-acceptance are fundamental steps in reclaiming a healthy relationship with food and body.

The Role of Compassion in Self-Nutritional Therapy
Compassion serves as the cornerstone of self-nutritional therapy. This involves treating oneself with kindness, gentleness, and understanding. Just as one would offer support and encouragement to a friend, individuals must extend the same level of compassion to themselves. When faced with moments of perceived "mistakes" or challenges in their nutritional journey, practicing self-compassion allows for growth and self-improvement without judgment.

Embracing Progress, Not Perfection
It's important to recognize that the journey of self-nutritional therapy is not linear, nor is it about achieving perfection. Rather, it's about progress, growth, and the continual practice of self-awareness. There will be times when old habits resurface, emotions trigger overeating, or stress influences food choices. These moments are opportunities for self-reflection and learning, not reasons for self-criticism.

Self-Nutritional Therapy Beyond Food
The practices of mindful eating and intuitive nutrition extend beyond food and mealtimes. They promote mindfulness and intentionality in various aspects of life. By

embracing the principles of self-awareness, presence, and non-judgment, individuals can apply these practices to relationships, work, and self-care activities. This holistic approach fosters a sense of balance, authenticity, and well-being.

Creating Lasting Change

The journey of self-nutritional therapy is an ongoing process that invites individuals to continually deepen their understanding of themselves and their relationship with food. By integrating mindful eating and intuitive nutrition into their lives, individuals can create lasting change that transcends fad diets and quick fixes. This change is rooted in self-empowerment, self-love, and the recognition that they possess the capacity to nourish their bodies and minds in a way that promotes holistic well-being.

A Nourished Mind and Spirit

As the chapter concludes, it emphasizes that self-nutritional therapy is not a destination but a lifelong journey—one that celebrates the intersection of nutrition, mindfulness, self-compassion, and holistic well-being. By becoming their own nutritional therapists, individuals embrace the power to transform their relationship with food, cultivate emotional resilience, and nourish their minds and spirits. This journey is an act of self-care, self-discovery, and self-love that paves the way to a life imbued with vitality, authenticity, and a deep connection to nourishment in all its forms.

Chapter 8: Your Kitchen Haven - Setting Up Your Culinary Space to Support Mental Health-Focused Cooking

The kitchen is more than just a place to prepare meals; it's a sanctuary where the alchemy of nourishment takes place. Chapter 8 delves into the concept of the kitchen as a haven, a space that plays a pivotal role in supporting mental health-focused cooking. From the arrangement of utensils to the choice of colors, this chapter explores how the design, organization, and ambiance of the kitchen can enhance the culinary journey, promote mindfulness, and foster emotional well-being.

Designing for Inspiration and Efficiency

A well-designed kitchen sets the stage for an enjoyable cooking experience. A clutter-free and organized space can alleviate stress and create a sense of control. Essential utensils and ingredients should be within easy reach, minimizing the need to search and creating an efficient flow during meal preparation. Adequate counter space and well-placed appliances allow for smooth movement and engagement with the cooking process.

Colors and Mood Elevation

Color has a profound impact on mood and emotions. The choice of colors in the kitchen can influence feelings of warmth, calmness, and even appetite stimulation. Soft and muted tones evoke tranquility, while vibrant colors like red can energize and stimulate creativity. Incorporating colors that resonate with positive emotions can create an inviting atmosphere that promotes mental wellness and a positive relationship with food.

Natural Light and Connection to Nature

Natural light is a powerful mood enhancer. A kitchen bathed in sunlight fosters a sense of well-being and connection to the outdoors. Large windows or strategically placed mirrors can amplify the impact of natural light. Additionally, potted herbs or small plants on windowsills introduce a touch of nature to the kitchen, infusing it with vitality and a sense of growth.

Mindful Cooking Spaces

Mindful cooking involves being present in the moment, engaging the senses, and savoring each step of the culinary process. Designing a kitchen that supports mindfulness requires creating spaces that encourage focus and sensory engagement. An uncluttered countertop, comfortable seating for tasting, and the incorporation of aromatherapy through herbs and essential oils can all contribute to a mindful cooking experience.

Kitchen as Creative Expression
Cooking is a form of creative expression, and the kitchen serves as the canvas. Personalizing the kitchen with artwork, photographs, or objects that evoke positive memories can foster a sense of creativity and inspiration. Customizing the space to reflect one's personality and preferences transforms the act of cooking into an opportunity for self-expression and emotional fulfillment.

Promoting Kitchen Wellness Rituals: Nurturing Mind, Body, and Spirit
In the bustling modern world, the kitchen has the potential to be more than just a utilitarian space for meal preparation; it can become a sanctuary for holistic well-being. Chapter 8 introduces the concept of "Promoting Kitchen Wellness Rituals," exploring how mindful practices integrated into the culinary routine can elevate the cooking experience to a transformative ritual. By infusing mindfulness, intentionality, and self-care into every aspect of the cooking process, individuals create a space where food preparation becomes a deeply nourishing practice for the mind, body, and spirit.

The Mindful Path to the Kitchen
Mindfulness, often associated with meditation and deep breathing, can extend its embrace to the kitchen. Before entering the culinary domain, taking a moment to center oneself can set the tone for a focused and present cooking experience. This can involve a few deep breaths or a brief

meditation, allowing individuals to release distractions and engage fully with the task at hand.

Setting Positive Intentions

Before embarking on the culinary journey, setting positive intentions can transform the act of cooking into a mindful and purposeful endeavor. These intentions can range from nourishing oneself and loved ones with wholesome food to infusing joy and creativity into the process. By anchoring the cooking experience with intentions, individuals create a framework for meaningful engagement with their culinary artistry.

Embracing Gratitude

Gratitude is a powerful emotion that can enhance the connection to the food being prepared and the overall cooking experience. Taking a moment to express gratitude for the ingredients, the hands that cultivated them, and the opportunity to nourish oneself can elevate the act of cooking to a practice of thankfulness and presence.

Sensory Engagement: A Mindful Symphony

Cooking engages the senses in a symphony of colors, aromas, textures, and flavors. Fostering sensory engagement transforms the kitchen into a haven of mindfulness. As ingredients are chopped, sautéed, and combined, savoring the visual and olfactory sensations brings the mind into the present moment, heightening the appreciation for the culinary journey.

The Rhythm of Movement

Cooking involves a dance of movement, from chopping and stirring to tasting and plating. Embracing this rhythm mindfully, with each action guided by intention, creates a seamless flow. As individuals immerse themselves in the rhythm of cooking, they are able to connect deeply with the process and let go of distractions.

Tasting as an Act of Mindfulness

Tasting is not merely a step in the cooking process; it's an act of mindfulness that deepens the connection to the food being prepared. Engaging all the senses in tasting—the colors, textures, aromas, and flavors—creates a sensory feast. Being fully present while tasting allows individuals to adjust seasonings, appreciate the subtleties, and acknowledge the transformation of ingredients into a nourishing creation.

Culinary Mindfulness as a Daily Ritual

Promoting kitchen wellness rituals involves cultivating mindfulness as a daily practice, rather than an occasional endeavor. Infusing mindfulness into cooking routines turns every meal preparation into an opportunity for self-care and self-discovery. As individuals engage in mindful cooking, they are not only nourishing their bodies but also cultivating emotional well-being, creativity, and a profound connection to the act of nourishment.

A Sanctuary of Self-Nourishment

As the chapter unfolds, it underscores that the concept of promoting kitchen wellness rituals is not about adding complexity to the cooking process. Instead, it's about transforming everyday actions into intentional moments of self-nourishment. By weaving mindfulness, gratitude, and intentionality into the culinary experience, individuals create a kitchen that serves as a sanctuary—one where the preparation of meals becomes an act of self-love, a source of joy, and a means of fostering emotional equilibrium.

Elevating the Ordinary to the Extraordinary

In the world of kitchen wellness rituals, the ordinary becomes extraordinary. Simple acts like chopping vegetables or stirring a pot can be infused with intention, transforming them into meaningful actions. The kitchen becomes a canvas for mindful living, where each culinary creation is a reflection of the love and mindfulness invested in it.

Ripple Effects Beyond the Kitchen

The practice of promoting kitchen wellness rituals has ripple effects that extend beyond the confines of the kitchen. The mindfulness cultivated during cooking can permeate other areas of life, promoting a sense of presence, resilience, and appreciation for the moment. The intentionality and self-care woven into the culinary journey inspire individuals to carry these practices into daily activities, relationships, and self-nourishing rituals.

Creating a Positive Relationship with Food: Fostering Nourishment and Emotional Harmony
In the intricate landscape of mental well-being and nutritional health, the relationship with food plays a central role. Chapter 9 delves into the profound concept of "Creating a Positive Relationship with Food," exploring how one's attitudes, beliefs, and interactions with food can significantly impact emotional equilibrium and overall well-being. By embracing mindful practices, self-compassion, and a holistic perspective, individuals can transform their relationship with food into one that nourishes both the body and the soul.

Food as More Than Fuel
Shifting the perception of food from mere sustenance to a source of pleasure, connection, and emotional nourishment is at the heart of cultivating a positive relationship with it. This perspective acknowledges the multi-faceted role of food—how it fuels the body while also serving as a medium for cultural traditions, social interactions, and self-expression.

Breaking Free from Diet Culture
The influence of diet culture, with its rigid rules and ideals, often shapes how individuals approach food. Creating a positive relationship with food requires breaking free from these restrictive narratives. Letting go of the dichotomy of "good" and "bad" foods and adopting an approach that embraces a wide variety of nourishing options is

fundamental to nourishing the mind and body without guilt or deprivation.

Mindful Eating as a Foundation

Mindful eating serves as a cornerstone in fostering a positive relationship with food. By practicing mindfulness during meals, individuals engage their senses, savor each bite, and cultivate a deep awareness of hunger and satiety cues. This approach encourages eating for pleasure, tuning into the body's signals, and letting go of external distractions that often disrupt the eating experience.

Listening to Body Wisdom

Honoring the body's innate wisdom is a pivotal aspect of a positive relationship with food. Tuning into hunger and fullness cues rather than adhering to external cues or societal norms empowers individuals to make choices that align with their bodies' needs. This practice not only supports physical well-being but also establishes a sense of trust and harmony between the individual and their body.

Mindful Decision-Making

Approaching food choices with mindfulness involves considering both nutritional needs and personal preferences. It means making decisions based on self-awareness, enjoyment, and nourishment. This mindful decision-making process avoids extremes and embraces moderation, allowing individuals to strike a balance between nourishing their bodies and savoring the pleasures of eating.

Self-Compassion in Nourishment
Creating a positive relationship with food requires cultivating self-compassion—a practice of treating oneself with kindness and understanding. This means letting go of self-criticism, guilt, and judgment associated with eating choices. Self-compassion acknowledges that food is an essential aspect of self-care and that occasional indulgences are natural and part of a balanced approach.

Embracing Food's Emotional Aspect
Food is intertwined with emotions and memories. It can serve as a source of comfort, celebration, and connection. Embracing the emotional aspect of food means allowing oneself to experience joy, pleasure, and satisfaction from eating without guilt. It's recognizing that enjoying a favorite treat or sharing a meal with loved ones is part of a holistic approach to well-being.

Cultivating a Sense of Empowerment
Creating a positive relationship with food is an act of empowerment. It involves consciously choosing foods that contribute to well-being, engaging in mindful eating practices, and nurturing a sense of respect for the body. This sense of empowerment transcends external influences and puts individuals in control of their choices, fostering a harmonious connection with nourishment.

A Journey of Exploration and Growth

As the chapter unfolds, it highlights that the journey toward a positive relationship with food is not linear but rather a path of exploration and growth. It's about learning to navigate different situations, addressing emotional triggers, and discovering what foods and eating patterns truly align with individual well-being. It's a journey that evolves as individuals become attuned to their bodies and cultivate a deep understanding of their unique needs.

Transformation Beyond the Plate

Creating a positive relationship with food has a transformative impact that extends far beyond the plate. It's not just about what is eaten but how it's approached—a shift from guilt and restriction to joy and self-compassion. This transformation influences not only physical health but also mental well-being, fostering emotional harmony, self-acceptance, and a deep sense of respect for the body's wisdom.

The Ritual of Cleanup and Closure

The culinary journey is not complete without the ritual of cleanup. Designing a space that facilitates easy cleanup—such as a well-organized sink and designated storage for cleaning supplies—ensures that the experience remains enjoyable from start to finish. This ritual of closure signifies the completion of a nourishing task and leaves the kitchen ready for the next culinary adventure.

Holistic Integration of the Kitchen and Well-Being

As the chapter concludes, it emphasizes that the kitchen is an integral part of the holistic approach to mental wellness through nutrition. Beyond its functional role, the kitchen becomes a reflection of one's values, intentions, and commitment to self-care. By designing a kitchen that aligns with mental health-focused cooking, individuals create a supportive environment that nourishes both body and mind. The kitchen haven becomes a space of transformation—a place where ingredients evolve into nourishing meals and the act of cooking becomes a journey of self-nourishment, creativity, and emotional well-being.

Chapter 9: The Holistic Six-Week Path - Your Step-by-Step Guide to a Nourished Mind and Resilient Spirit

Chapter 9 introduces readers to a transformative journey, the "Holistic Six-Week Path," designed to guide individuals towards a nourished mind and resilient spirit. This comprehensive approach integrates mindful eating, self-care practices, and emotional well-being strategies over the span of six weeks. By embracing this path, individuals can cultivate a harmonious relationship with food, nurture their mental health, and foster emotional equilibrium.

Week 1: Foundation of Mindful Awareness

The journey towards a nourished mind and resilient spirit begins with Week 1: the establishment of a strong foundation of mindful awareness. This foundational week sets the tone for the transformative path ahead, inviting individuals to delve into the intricacies of their relationship with food, body cues, and emotions. By practicing mindful eating, journaling, and body awareness, participants embark on a journey of self-discovery, aligning their actions with intentionality and presence.

Understanding Mindful Awareness

Mindful awareness is the practice of being fully present in the moment, without judgment or distraction. It involves engaging the senses and paying attention to the present experience. In the context of eating, mindful awareness encourages individuals to savor each bite, engage their senses, and cultivate a deeper connection to the nourishing act of consuming food.

Mindful Eating: A Journey of Sensory Exploration

During Week 1, participants explore mindful eating—a practice that encourages a new approach to meals. Instead of rushing through bites, individuals savor each mouthful, engaging all their senses. They notice the colors, aromas, textures, and flavors of their food. This heightened sensory experience fosters a deeper connection to the nourishment being received, transforming eating from a routine task to a mindful ritual.

Journaling: Reflection and Self-Discovery

Journaling becomes a valuable tool during Week 1, enabling participants to reflect on their eating habits, emotions, and triggers. By putting thoughts onto paper, individuals gain insights into their patterns of eating, emotions associated with food, and moments of mindless consumption. Journaling fosters self-awareness, providing a foundation for making mindful choices and addressing any challenges that arise.

Body Awareness: Tuning into Cues

Cultivating awareness of bodily cues is a central aspect of Week 1. Participants learn to recognize sensations of hunger and fullness, distinguishing between physical and emotional cues. By tuning into the body's signals, individuals can make eating decisions that are aligned with their true needs. This practice fosters a sense of respect for the body's wisdom and promotes mindful eating choices.

Embracing Challenges with Compassion
Week 1 also introduces the concept of self-compassion in the face of challenges. Participants may encounter moments of mindless eating, emotional triggers, or old habits resurfacing. Rather than responding with self-criticism, self-compassion encourages individuals to treat themselves with kindness and understanding. This shift in attitude lays the groundwork for a positive relationship with both food and oneself.

Creating Mindful Rituals
Throughout Week 1, participants are encouraged to create mindful rituals around eating. This may involve setting a designated eating space, taking a few deep breaths before a meal, or expressing gratitude for the nourishment received. These rituals serve as reminders to engage in mindful eating practices, fostering a sense of presence and intentionality during meals.

Mindful Awareness as a Lifelong Skill
As the week concludes, the significance of mindful awareness is highlighted as a lifelong skill. While Week 1 serves as an introduction, the practice of mindful eating and awareness can continue to evolve and deepen. By

embracing mindful eating as a foundational practice, individuals equip themselves with a powerful tool that can be integrated into their daily lives, promoting a sense of presence, mindfulness, and connection to the nourishment they receive.

A Mindful Beginning

The conclusion of Week 1 marks a powerful beginning on the journey towards a nourished mind and resilient spirit. By cultivating mindful awareness of eating habits, body cues, and emotions, participants lay the groundwork for transformative change. This week establishes a solid foundation, equipping individuals with the tools to navigate the complex landscape of nutrition and emotional well-being with intentionality, presence, and compassion.

Week 2: Nourishing Self-Compassion

As the journey towards a nourished mind and resilient spirit continues, Week 2 brings the spotlight to the essential theme of self-compassion. This week is dedicated to fostering a deep sense of self-kindness, understanding, and acceptance—a vital aspect of creating a positive relationship with food and nurturing emotional well-being. Through the practices of positive self-talk, self-affirmations, and releasing self-judgment, participants embark on a transformative exploration of self-compassion.

Understanding Self-Compassion

Self-compassion involves treating oneself with the same kindness and understanding that one would extend to a friend in times of difficulty. It's a practice of acknowledging one's imperfections and challenges without judgment, while offering support and nurturing. In the context of the relationship with food, self-compassion helps individuals break free from the cycle of guilt and shame often associated with eating choices.

Embracing Positive Self-Talk

During Week 2, participants begin to pay attention to their inner dialogue. Positive self-talk involves challenging and reframing negative thoughts related to eating and body image. Instead of criticizing themselves for indulging or making certain food choices, participants learn to speak to themselves with encouragement and understanding. This shift in self-talk cultivates an environment of self-compassion and self-acceptance.

Cultivating Self-Affirmations

Week 2 encourages individuals to develop self-affirmations—positive statements that uplift and empower. These affirmations are personalized and focus on self-compassion, body positivity, and emotional well-being. By repeating these affirmations regularly, participants nourish their self-esteem, reinforcing the practice of self-compassion as a foundational aspect of their journey.

Releasing the Chains of Self-Judgment
A significant aspect of Week 2 is releasing the chains of self-judgment. Participants learn to recognize moments when self-criticism arises, particularly in relation to eating habits and body image. They practice gently redirecting these judgmental thoughts towards self-compassionate perspectives. This practice helps individuals free themselves from the burden of unrealistic expectations and fosters emotional healing.

Embracing Imperfections with Kindness
Self-compassion invites individuals to embrace their imperfections and challenges with kindness. This includes acknowledging that everyone has moments of overindulgence, emotional eating, or lapses in mindful eating. Instead of berating themselves, participants learn to treat these moments with self-kindness, understanding that they are part of the human experience.

Nurturing Emotional Healing
Week 2 also acknowledges that food choices can be intertwined with emotions and stress. Participants learn that self-compassion serves as a soothing balm during times of emotional turbulence. By offering themselves understanding and support, individuals can navigate challenging emotions without turning to food for comfort.

Self-Compassion as a Lifelong Practice

The importance of self-compassion extends beyond Week 2—it's a lifelong practice that supports emotional well-being and self-acceptance. The practices introduced during this week lay the foundation for ongoing self-compassion, allowing individuals to face challenges with a kind heart, cultivate a positive relationship with food, and develop a sense of emotional resilience.

Embracing Transformation and Growth

As the week comes to an end, participants have begun to experience the transformational power of self-compassion. The practices of positive self-talk, self-affirmations, and releasing self-judgment create an environment of self-nurturing and growth. By fostering a deep sense of self-compassion, individuals are better equipped to navigate the complexities of their relationship with food, promoting a positive attitude towards eating and a foundation of emotional well-being.

Nourishing the Heart and Soul

Week 2 highlights that self-compassion is an essential ingredient in the recipe for a nourished mind and resilient spirit. By embracing self-kindness, understanding, and acceptance, individuals create an inner landscape that supports not only their relationship with food but also their emotional health. This week marks a pivotal step towards fostering a positive relationship with both food and oneself—a journey that promotes emotional harmony, self-love, and a deep sense of well-being.

Week 3: Embracing Nutrient-Rich Nourishment - Fueling Body and Mind

In Week 3 of your transformative journey towards a nourished mind and resilient spirit, the spotlight is on the significance of nutrient-rich nourishment. This week, you delve into the profound connection between your food choices and their impact on both cognitive function and emotional well-being. As you explore this theme, you'll uncover the essential nutrients that support mental health, discover their sources, and learn how to create meals that prioritize your brain's health and emotional equilibrium.

Understanding Nutrient-Rich Nourishment

At the heart of Week 3 lies the concept of nutrient-rich nourishment. This approach revolves around selecting foods that not only tantalize your taste buds but are also abundant in essential vitamins, minerals, and antioxidants. By opting for nutrient-dense foods, you're choosing to fuel your body and mind with the elements they need to thrive.

Essential Nutrients for Mental Health

Week 3 guides you through a journey of understanding the specific nutrients that play a crucial role in supporting your mental health. Among these are:

1. Omega-3 Fatty Acids: These healthy fats are renowned for their cognitive benefits. Found in fatty fish like salmon, mackerel, and sardines, as well as in walnuts and flaxseeds, omega-3 fatty acids contribute to brain health and mood regulation.

2. B Vitamins: Certain B vitamins, such as B6, B9 (folate), and B12, are associated with mood regulation and cognitive function. You can find them in whole grains, leafy greens, legumes, nuts, seeds, and animal products.

3. Antioxidants: Foods rich in antioxidants, such as berries, dark leafy greens, and colorful vegetables, protect your brain cells from oxidative stress and inflammation, which can contribute to cognitive decline.

4. Magnesium: This mineral supports relaxation and stress management. Leafy greens, nuts, seeds, whole grains, and dark chocolate are excellent sources of magnesium.

Mindful Nutrition: A Balanced Approach
Week 3 emphasizes that nutrient-rich nourishment isn't about restrictive diets or counting calories. It's about embracing a balanced and holistic approach to eating. By

incorporating a colorful variety of whole foods into your meals, you ensure that you receive a spectrum of essential nutrients that contribute to your overall well-being.

Crafting Brain-Boosting Meals

To practically apply the principles of Week 3, you're introduced to brain-boosting recipes that are both delicious and nutritious. These recipes emphasize the inclusion of ingredients rich in the aforementioned nutrients. For instance:

A salmon salad featuring omega-3-rich salmon fillets, leafy greens, colorful vegetables, and a sprinkle of nuts for added crunch and magnesium.

A vibrant smoothie bowl made with antioxidant-packed berries, leafy greens, and a handful of nuts or seeds for omega-3s.

Mindful Consumption of Nutrients

During this week, you're encouraged to engage in mindful consumption of nutrients. Pay attention to how different foods make you feel physically and emotionally. By cultivating this awareness, you can make informed choices that contribute to your cognitive function, mood, and energy levels.

Sustaining Nutrient-Rich Habits

Week 3 sets the foundation for a sustained commitment to nutrient-rich nourishment. The practices you explore are not meant to be temporary but rather a lifelong approach to eating. By consistently incorporating brain-boosting nutrients into your diet, you equip yourself with the tools to support both your mental health and your overall well-being.

A Nutrient-Rich Path Forward

As the week concludes, you've gained a deeper appreciation for the impact of nutrient-rich nourishment on your mind and body. You've explored the essential nutrients that play a pivotal role in supporting cognitive function and emotional balance. By making mindful choices and embracing nutrient-dense foods, you're actively nurturing a nourished mind and resilient spirit—a journey that speaks volumes about your commitment to holistic well-being.

Week 4: Exploring Mindful Cooking Rituals

As the journey towards a nourished mind and resilient spirit continues, Week 4 invites participants to embark on a culinary exploration of mindful cooking rituals. This week is dedicated to transforming the act of cooking into a mindful and intentional practice—a creative endeavor that fosters a deep connection to the ingredients, the process, and the nourishment being prepared. By infusing each step with mindfulness and presence, participants not only create delicious meals but also cultivate a sense of joy, creativity, and emotional well-being.

Understanding Mindful Cooking Rituals

Mindful cooking rituals involve approaching the act of cooking with intentionality, awareness, and a sense of presence. It's about shifting from a hurried routine to an immersive experience where every chop, stir, and sizzle becomes an opportunity for mindfulness. Mindful cooking encourages individuals to engage their senses, savor the moment, and express creativity through culinary artistry.

Creating a Mindful Kitchen Space

During Week 4, participants begin by creating a mindful kitchen space—a environment that supports mindful cooking rituals. This involves decluttering the cooking area, organizing utensils, and creating a space that promotes ease and flow. The mindful kitchen becomes a sanctuary for culinary creativity and self-expression.

Engaging the Senses**

Mindful cooking involves engaging all the senses in the culinary experience. Participants are encouraged to explore the colors, textures, aromas, and sounds of the ingredients they are working with. This sensory engagement brings a heightened awareness to the cooking process, fostering a deeper connection to the art of nourishment.

Savoring the Process

Week 4 emphasizes the importance of savoring the cooking process itself, rather than just focusing on the end result.

Participants are encouraged to slow down, take deliberate actions, and appreciate each step—from chopping vegetables to simmering sauces. This practice cultivates a sense of mindfulness and presence in the kitchen.

Cultivating Creativity and Joy

Mindful cooking rituals provide an avenue for culinary creativity and joy. Participants are encouraged to experiment with flavors, textures, and ingredients, embracing the artistry of cooking. This creative exploration not only enhances the flavor of the dishes but also promotes emotional well-being through self-expression.

Bringing Mindfulness to Ingredients

Mindful cooking involves developing a connection to the ingredients themselves. Participants are encouraged to reflect on where the ingredients come from, how they were grown or produced, and the journey they took to reach the kitchen. This practice fosters gratitude and a sense of interconnectedness with the food being prepared.

Mindful Meal Preparation

Week 4 also introduces the concept of mindful meal preparation. This involves setting aside dedicated time to cook without distractions. Participants practice being fully present in the cooking process, letting go of external concerns and immersing themselves in the act of nourishment.

Nourishing the Soul Through Cooking

As the week unfolds, participants discover that mindful cooking rituals are not just about the food—they're about nurturing the soul. The act of preparing meals becomes a form of self-care, an avenue for creativity, and an expression of love for oneself and others.

Mindful Cooking as a Lifestyle
Week 4 highlights that mindful cooking is not confined to a specific time frame—it's a lifestyle that can be integrated into daily routines. By embracing mindful cooking rituals, participants create a daily practice of presence, joy, and self-expression that supports their overall well-being.

Cultivating Mindful Culinary Rituals
As the week concludes, participants have experienced the transformative power of mindful cooking rituals. They've learned that cooking is not just a chore but an opportunity for mindfulness, creativity, and emotional well-being. By infusing each culinary creation with intention and presence, participants create meals that nourish not only the body but also the mind and spirit, fostering a profound connection to the nourishing journey of mindful cooking.

Week 5: Emotional Resilience Through Movement
As the journey toward a nourished mind and resilient spirit continues, Week 5 introduces the transformative theme of "Emotional Resilience Through Movement." This week focuses on the profound impact of physical activity on

emotional well-being. Participants explore how movement, whether through yoga, walking, dancing, or other forms of exercise, can become a powerful tool for managing stress, enhancing mood, and promoting emotional resilience.

Understanding the Mind-Body Connection

Week 5 acknowledges the intricate connection between the mind and body. Physical activity has been shown to release endorphins, the body's natural mood enhancers, and reduce levels of stress hormones. By engaging in movement, individuals can create a positive feedback loop where physical well-being supports emotional well-being and vice versa.

Exploring Movement Modalities

Participants in Week 5 have the opportunity to explore various movement modalities that resonate with them. This could range from gentle yoga and stretching routines to more vigorous activities like running or dancing. The emphasis is on choosing activities that bring joy, relaxation, and a sense of flow.

Yoga: Nurturing Mindfulness and Flexibility

Yoga is a prominent focus of Week 5 due to its dual benefits of enhancing both physical and emotional well-being. Yoga combines mindful movement with deep breathing, promoting relaxation and a sense of presence. The practice also enhances flexibility, balance, and strength, contributing to physical vitality and emotional resilience.

Walking: Finding Peace in Motion
Walking serves as a simple yet powerful form of movement that fosters emotional resilience. Whether it's a leisurely stroll through nature or a brisk walk in the neighborhood, walking promotes relaxation, reduces stress, and clears the mind. Week 5 encourages participants to embrace walking as a mindfulness practice.

Dance: Expressing Emotions Through Movement
For those who enjoy more expressive forms of movement, dance becomes a valuable tool for emotional resilience. Dancing allows individuals to channel and release emotions through physical expression. Whether it's dancing alone in the living room or joining a dance class, Week 5 encourages participants to dance their way to emotional well-being.

Mindful Movement: A Path to Presence
Mindful movement is a central theme of Week 5. Participants are guided to approach movement as a form of meditation, focusing on the sensations, breath, and rhythm of their bodies. This mindful approach enhances the emotional benefits of movement, fostering a sense of calm and presence.

Creating a Movement Routine
Week 5 emphasizes the importance of creating a sustainable movement routine. Instead of viewing exercise as a chore,

participants are encouraged to view it as a form of self-care. By selecting activities they enjoy and incorporating movement into their daily schedules, individuals make emotional resilience an integral part of their lives.

Enhancing Mood and Emotional Resilience

As participants engage in movement throughout the week, they begin to experience the positive effects on their mood and emotional resilience. Physical activity has the ability to reduce symptoms of anxiety and depression, promote relaxation, and enhance overall emotional well-being.

Movement as a Lifelong Practice

Week 5's teachings extend beyond its timeframe. The practices introduced during this week are meant to cultivate a lifelong relationship with movement as a means of nurturing emotional resilience. By embracing physical activity as an essential aspect of self-care, individuals set themselves on a path to sustained emotional well-being.

A Resilient Mind and Body

As the week concludes, participants have not only explored the connection between movement and emotional resilience but have also experienced its effects firsthand. By incorporating movement into their lives, they've discovered a powerful tool for managing stress, enhancing mood, and fostering emotional well-being. Week 5 marks a significant step on the journey towards a nourished mind and resilient spirit—a journey where movement becomes a source of strength, balance, and emotional vitality.

Week 6: Cultivating Mind-Body Harmony

As the transformative journey towards a nourished mind and resilient spirit reaches its culmination, Week 6 is dedicated to the theme of "Cultivating Mind-Body Harmony." This week serves as a synthesis of the practices and insights gained throughout the preceding weeks. Participants are encouraged to integrate the lessons of mindful awareness, self-compassion, nutrient-rich nourishment, mindful cooking, and movement into a cohesive and holistic approach to well-being.

The Holistic Approach

Week 6 underscores the holistic nature of well-being, where the mind, body, and spirit are interconnected and influence each other. The practices introduced throughout the journey are not isolated; they come together to form a comprehensive framework for promoting emotional and mental wellness.

Mindful Awareness as the Foundation

Participants revisit the mindful awareness practices introduced in Week 1. This serves as a reminder that being present and attentive in daily life is fundamental to well-being. The cultivation of mindful awareness continues to be a cornerstone practice for nurturing emotional equilibrium and fostering a positive relationship with food.

Self-Compassion: A Supportive Ally
Week 6 reinforces the practice of self-compassion as an ongoing source of support. Participants are encouraged to continue treating themselves with kindness and understanding, particularly in moments of challenge or setback. Self-compassion serves as a buffer against self-criticism and reinforces a healthy self-image.

Nutrient-Rich Nourishment as Nourishment for the Mind
The connection between nutrition and emotional well-being is revisited in Week 6. Participants are invited to sustain the practice of choosing nutrient-rich foods that support cognitive function and mood regulation. By recognizing the impact of food choices on mental health, individuals are empowered to prioritize their nourishment.

Mindful Cooking as Self-Care
Mindful cooking rituals, introduced in Week 4, continue to be a means of self-care and creativity. Participants are encouraged to maintain a connection to the act of cooking, infusing meals with intention and mindfulness. The practice of mindful cooking becomes an expression of self-love and a source of emotional nourishment.

Movement as a Way of Life
The lessons of Week 5's focus on movement are integrated into daily life during Week 6. Participants are encouraged to establish a sustainable movement routine that supports emotional resilience and physical vitality. Whether it's yoga, walking, dance, or any other form of exercise, movement becomes an integral part of their lifestyle.

Holistic Well-Being in Daily Life
Week 6 invites participants to weave the practices of the past weeks into their daily lives. Mindful awareness informs eating habits, self-compassion guides inner dialogue, nutrient-rich nourishment fuels cognitive function, mindful cooking promotes creativity, and movement nurtures emotional well-being. This integration fosters a sense of balance and harmony in daily routines.

Reflection and Celebration
As the transformative journey comes to a close, participants are encouraged to reflect on their progress and celebrate their achievements. The cultivation of a nourished mind and resilient spirit is not a linear process; it involves growth, setbacks, and continuous learning. Reflecting on the journey allows individuals to recognize their resilience and commitment to well-being.

Continued Growth and Well-Being
Week 6 is not an endpoint but a stepping stone to continued growth and well-being. The practices and principles

introduced throughout the journey are meant to be carried forward into daily life. By embracing a holistic approach to well-being—one that encompasses mindful awareness, self-compassion, nourishment, creativity, and movement—participants set themselves on a path of sustained emotional and mental wellness.

A Nourished Mind and Resilient Spirit
As the journey concludes, participants have experienced a profound transformation. Through the integration of mindful practices, self-care, and holistic well-being, they've cultivated a nourished mind and a resilient spirit. Week 6 marks the beginning of an ongoing journey—one that is characterized by self-discovery, growth, and a deep commitment to the nourishing path of well-being.

The Holistic Six-Week Path as a Lifelong Journey
The beauty of the Holistic Six-Week Path lies in its adaptability and sustainability. While the path is designed to be completed in six weeks, its principles can be incorporated into daily life as ongoing practices. The journey doesn't end at Week 6; rather, it lays the groundwork for a lifelong commitment to nourishing the mind, body, and spirit through mindfulness, self-compassion, and holistic well-being.

Personal Transformation and Empowerment
By following the Holistic Six-Week Path, individuals embark on a journey of personal transformation and

empowerment. The path is not a rigid prescription but a flexible framework that invites individuals to explore, reflect, and adapt practices to their unique needs. Through this journey, participants become their own agents of change, empowered to navigate challenges, celebrate successes, and cultivate a lifelong commitment to mental wellness through nutrition.

Charting Your Ongoing Path

As the chapter concludes, it encourages readers to chart their ongoing path of growth and self-discovery. The Holistic Six-Week Path is a springboard for continued exploration, offering a roadmap to navigate the complexities of nourishment and mental well-being. By integrating mindful practices, self-compassion, and holistic principles into daily life, individuals can create a life that radiates vitality, emotional resilience, and a deep connection to the nourishing journey of self-discovery.

Chapter 10: Culinary Therapy: Recipes for Restoration

In the journey towards a nourished mind and resilient spirit, food becomes not only sustenance but also a form of therapy. Chapter 10 invites you to explore the realm of culinary therapy—a practice that leverages the healing power of nutrient-packed, delicious meals to support your mental well-being. Through carefully crafted recipes that prioritize brain health, mood regulation, and emotional equilibrium, this chapter empowers you to use food as a tool for restoration and healing.

Understanding Culinary Therapy
Culinary therapy goes beyond the realm of conventional nutrition. It recognizes that the act of preparing and enjoying nourishing meals can be a source of comfort, joy, and healing. This practice emphasizes the integration of mindful cooking, nutrient-rich ingredients, and mindful consumption to foster emotional resilience and mental healing.

Recipes for Brain Health and Emotional Well-Being
Chapter 10 presents a collection of recipes that are thoughtfully designed to promote brain health and support emotional well-being. Each recipe is crafted with a combination of ingredients that provide essential nutrients

for cognitive function, mood regulation, and stress management.

1. Brain-Boosting Breakfast Smoothie:
This vibrant concoction sets the tone for your day with a symphony of flavors and nutrients. Blueberries and strawberries offer a burst of antioxidants, protecting your brain cells from oxidative stress. Omega-3-rich chia seeds support cognitive function, while the greens provide a wealth of vitamins and minerals. Greek yogurt adds a creamy texture and a probiotic punch, promoting gut health, which in turn influences mood regulation.

2. Salmon and Quinoa Power Bowl:
Lunch becomes a delightful journey with this power bowl that encapsulates diverse textures and flavors. Omega-3 fatty acids from salmon bolster brain health by promoting optimal neurotransmitter function. Protein-packed quinoa provides sustained energy and essential amino acids, contributing to neurotransmitter production. The medley of colorful vegetables ensures a spectrum of vitamins and minerals that play pivotal roles in cognitive well-being.

3. Mood-Boosting Turmeric Omelette:
Revitalize your mood with this omelette infused with the golden touch of turmeric. Curcumin, the active compound in turmeric, exhibits anti-inflammatory and antioxidant properties, supporting brain health and mood regulation.

Protein from eggs provides the building blocks for neurotransmitters, while B vitamins contribute to the synthesis of mood-enhancing chemicals.

4. Nutrient-Dense Avocado Toast:
A modern classic takes on new dimensions of nutrition. Creamy avocados offer healthy fats that nourish your brain cells, promoting cognitive function and emotional stability. Chia seeds and flaxseeds provide omega-3s, reinforcing brain health. Pumpkin seeds sprinkle a touch of magnesium and zinc, essential minerals that contribute to emotional well-being.

5. Quinoa and Veggie Stuffed Bell Peppers:
Dinnertime becomes a celebration of colors and nutrients with these stuffed bell peppers. Quinoa, a complete protein source, provides amino acids necessary for neurotransmitter synthesis. Lean protein from ground turkey or tofu supports mood stability. The assortment of vegetables contributes an array of vitamins, minerals, and antioxidants that bolster brain health and emotional resilience.

6. Blissful Berry Parfait:
Indulgence meets nutrition in this guilt-free dessert. Antioxidant-rich berries combat oxidative stress, enhancing brain function and protecting against cognitive decline. Probiotic-rich Greek yogurt supports gut-brain communication, influencing mood and emotional

regulation. Nuts offer a satisfying crunch and a dose of omega-3 fatty acids that promote overall mental well-being.

7. Bountiful Spinach and Walnut Salad:
This salad is not just a feast for the eyes but a gift to your brain. Spinach, a leafy green powerhouse, boasts an abundance of vitamins and minerals crucial for cognitive function. Omega-3-rich walnuts support brain health and enhance mood. Mandarin oranges contribute a touch of sweetness and vitamin C, a nutrient that aids in neurotransmitter production.

8. Energizing Trail Mix:
Customize your mood-enhancing snack with this energizing trail mix. Almonds provide magnesium, a mineral that contributes to stress reduction and mood stability. Pumpkin seeds offer zinc, which plays a role in neurotransmitter function. Dried cranberries add a touch of sweetness while contributing antioxidants that support brain health.

9. Wholesome Chickpea Stir-Fry:
In the whirlwind of modern life, this stir-fry stands as a testament to both nutrition and convenience. Chickpeas supply B vitamins and fiber that support cognitive function and gut health. A kaleidoscope of vegetables offers vitamins and minerals that contribute to emotional equilibrium. The savory stir-fry sauce adds depth of flavor and nourishment.

10. Hearty Lentil and Vegetable Soup:
As the sun sets, this hearty soup envelops you in warmth
and nourishment. Lentils provide a plant-based protein
source rich in essential amino acids that support
neurotransmitter synthesis. An ensemble of vegetables
contributes a rainbow of vitamins, minerals, and
antioxidants that bolster brain health and emotional well-
being.

11. Mediterranean Quinoa Salad:
Transport your taste buds to the shores of the Mediterranean
with this vibrant salad. Quinoa serves as a protein-rich base,
supporting neurotransmitter synthesis. Olive oil, a staple of
the Mediterranean diet, provides healthy fats that nourish
brain cells. Fresh vegetables, feta cheese, and a sprinkle of
herbs offer an array of vitamins and minerals that promote
cognitive function and emotional balance.

12. Dark Chocolate Berry Bark:
Indulge in a treat that's not only delicious but also offers
brain-boosting benefits. Dark chocolate contains flavonoids
that enhance blood flow to the brain, improving cognitive
function. This bark combines antioxidant-rich berries with
the richness of dark chocolate, creating a delightful
combination that supports brain health and elevates mood.

13. Herbed Grilled Chicken with Quinoa Pilaf:
Savor the flavors of herbs and protein in this wholesome
dish. Grilled chicken provides lean protein necessary for

neurotransmitter production. Quinoa pilaf offers a blend of essential nutrients, including B vitamins and amino acids, that contribute to cognitive health. The dish is rounded out with a variety of vegetables that add vitamins and minerals to your plate.

14. Sweet Potato and Black Bean Tacos:

Experience a fiesta of flavors and nutrients with these tacos. Sweet potatoes offer complex carbohydrates that provide sustained energy for your brain. Black beans supply a combination of fiber and protein that support gut health and neurotransmitter synthesis. Avocado adds healthy fats that promote cognitive function.

15. Walnut and Banana Overnight Oats:

Begin your day with a jar of creamy overnight oats enriched with brain-boosting ingredients. Omega-3-rich walnuts provide anti-inflammatory benefits that support cognitive health. Bananas offer potassium and other nutrients that enhance brain function. Oats provide a steady release of energy, sustaining you throughout the morning.

16. Seared Tofu and Vegetable Stir-Fry:

Embrace the benefits of plant-based nutrition with this colorful stir-fry. Seared tofu serves as a protein source that supports neurotransmitter synthesis. A variety of vegetables contributes an array of vitamins, minerals, and antioxidants that enhance cognitive function and emotional well-being. A flavorful stir-fry sauce ties the dish together.

17. Berry and Almond Butter Stuffed Dates:
Delight in a snack that marries the sweetness of dates with the richness of almond butter and the vibrancy of berries. Dates provide natural sweetness along with fiber that supports gut health. Almond butter offers healthy fats that nourish brain cells. Berries add antioxidants that protect brain health.

18. Broccoli and Spinach Frittata:
Elevate your brunch with a frittata that's as nutritious as it is flavorful. Broccoli and spinach offer a wealth of vitamins and minerals that contribute to cognitive function. Eggs provide protein and B vitamins that support mood regulation. This frittata becomes a celebration of color, taste, and well-being.

19. Mixed Berry Chia Pudding:
Indulge in the creaminess of chia pudding adorned with a medley of mixed berries. Chia seeds provide omega-3 fatty acids and fiber that support brain health and gut function. Berries offer antioxidants that protect brain cells from oxidative stress. This dessert-like pudding becomes a nourishing treat for your mind.

20. Apple Cinnamon Quinoa Breakfast Bowl:
Wrap up your culinary journey with a comforting breakfast bowl that exudes warmth and nourishment. Quinoa provides protein and essential amino acids that support neurotransmitter synthesis. Apples offer fiber and nutrients

that enhance cognitive function. Cinnamon adds a touch of warmth and anti-inflammatory benefits.

21. Blueberry and Almond Spinach Salad:
Revitalize your palate with a salad that's both refreshing and brain-boosting. Blueberries offer a burst of antioxidants that protect brain cells from damage. Almonds provide healthy fats and vitamin E, contributing to cognitive health. Spinach adds a dose of folate, a B vitamin associated with mood regulation.

22. Herbed Quinoa Stuffed Mushrooms:
Elevate your appetizer game with these stuffed mushrooms that pack a nutritional punch. Quinoa serves as a plant-based protein source that supports neurotransmitter function. Fresh herbs add flavor and anti-inflammatory benefits, enhancing brain health. The mushrooms themselves are rich in B vitamins and minerals that contribute to cognitive well-being.

23. Orange and Ginger Glazed Salmon:
Experience a fusion of flavors that promote brain health with this salmon dish. Omega-3 fatty acids from salmon support cognitive function and mood regulation. Oranges provide vitamin C, an antioxidant that protects brain cells. Ginger adds a touch of warmth and anti-inflammatory properties.

24. Citrus and Avocado Quinoa Salad:
Savor the harmonious blend of citrusy and creamy flavors in this quinoa salad. Citrus fruits provide vitamin C and antioxidants that bolster brain health. Avocado contributes healthy fats that nourish brain cells and support cognitive function. Quinoa serves as a foundation of protein and essential amino acids.

25. Banana Walnut Muffins:
End your culinary journey with a treat that's both delightful and nutritious. Bananas offer potassium and vitamins that enhance brain function. Walnuts provide omega-3 fatty acids and antioxidants that promote cognitive health. These muffins are a testament to the idea that indulgence can be coupled with nourishment.

Mindful Cooking for Healing
Incorporating mindful cooking into these recipes amplifies their therapeutic benefits. As you engage in each step of preparation, you infuse the meal with intention, presence, and creativity. Mindful cooking elevates the experience from mere sustenance to a form of self-care and emotional restoration.

Mindful Consumption: Nourishing Your Body and Mind

Just as important as the cooking process is the act of mindful consumption. As you savor each bite of these nourishing dishes, engage your senses and pay attention to the flavors, textures, and nourishment they provide. Mindful consumption enhances the connection between food and emotional well-being.

The Healing Power of Food

Food has an incredible ability to transcend its role as mere sustenance, becoming a powerful source of healing for the mind, body, and soul. The concept of food as medicine is not new; cultures across the world have recognized the profound impact of what we consume on our overall well-being for centuries. In recent years, this idea has gained renewed attention, as scientific research continues to unveil the intricate connections between nutrition, brain health, and emotional well-being.

At the heart of the healing power of food lies the realization that every bite we take has the potential to influence our physical health and mental state. Nutrients found in the foods we consume play essential roles in supporting brain function, regulating mood, and promoting emotional resilience. Antioxidants protect brain cells from oxidative stress, omega-3 fatty acids support neurotransmitter function, and B vitamins contribute to mood regulation—all of which underscore the interplay between nutrition and mental wellness.

A Holistic Approach to Well-Being
The healing power of food extends beyond the biochemical interactions within our bodies. It encompasses the ritual of mindful cooking, the joy of sharing a meal with loved ones, and the connection between what we eat and how we feel. When we approach food with intention and mindfulness, we create a space for healing on a deeper level. The act of selecting fresh, nutrient-dense ingredients and transforming them into nourishing meals becomes a form of self-care and self-expression.

Moreover, the healing power of food is not confined to the physical realm. It also addresses the emotional and psychological aspects of our well-being. Comfort foods, for instance, have a unique way of soothing our souls, providing a sense of warmth and familiarity during times of stress or emotional turmoil. Sharing a meal with others fosters a sense of community and belonging, promoting feelings of happiness and contentment.

Culinary Therapy: A Journey to Wholeness
Culinary therapy, as explored in Chapter 10, encapsulates the profound connection between food and healing. It recognizes that the act of preparing and consuming meals can be therapeutic, serving as a form of self-expression, creativity, and self-nurturing. By mindfully selecting ingredients and engaging in the cooking process with intention, individuals can foster a deeper connection to their own well-being.

Through carefully curated recipes that prioritize brain health, emotional balance, and cognitive function, culinary therapy becomes a tangible practice. Each recipe is a canvas through which essential nutrients are woven into delectable creations. As you prepare and enjoy these dishes, you're not just nourishing your body; you're also engaging in a form of self-care that contributes to your mental and emotional vitality.

Embracing Culinary Therapy
As you embrace the recipes and practices of culinary therapy, you're taking a proactive step towards self-care and mental healing. With each carefully selected ingredient and each mindful moment spent in the kitchen, you're fostering a deeper connection to your own well-being. Chapter 10 invites you to experience the transformative potential of food, guiding you on a path of nourishment, restoration, and the cultivation of a nourished mind and resilient spirit.

Chapter 11: Elevate Your Plate, Elevate Your Mood

In the quest for mental wellness, the link between what you eat and how you feel becomes ever more evident. Chapter 11 serves as your guide to curating a plate that not only satisfies your taste buds but also elevates your mood and supports your emotional well-being. By harnessing the power of specific nutrients and food groups, this chapter empowers you to make informed choices that contribute to a more positive and resilient mental state.

Understanding Nutritional Mood Enhancement
The concept of "food as a mood enhancer" is rooted in the intricate interplay between the brain and the gut. The gut-brain connection, also known as the "second brain," demonstrates that the state of your gut can influence your emotional state. The gut microbiome—a collection of trillions of microorganisms living in your digestive tract—plays a pivotal role in this connection. Certain foods promote the growth of beneficial gut bacteria, which can then influence neurotransmitter production and mood-regulating pathways in the brain.

Within the intricate tapestry of human well-being, the connection between the foods we consume and our emotional state is a thread of profound significance. In Chapter 11, "Elevate Your Plate, Elevate Your Mood," the focus turns to the art of crafting meals that not only sustain us physically but also serve as allies in the pursuit of emotional equilibrium. The chapter unfurls a rich tapestry of nutrient-dense foods, each woven with a specific set of essential nutrients that play pivotal roles in brain health, neurotransmitter function, and the delicate dance of emotions.

The Nutritional Symphony: A Categorization of Mood-Enhancing Foods

The heart of this chapter lies in its comprehensive compilation of mood-enhancing foods, meticulously organized into categories that represent the diverse ways in which nutrients impact our mental well-being:

1. Omega-3 Fatty Acids: Nourishing the Neural Pathways

Omega-3 fatty acids, celebrated for their anti-inflammatory prowess, emerge as key players in brain health. Fatty fish, such as salmon, mackerel, and sardines, provide these valuable fats, which bolster cognitive function and neurotransmitter signaling. These fats, often deemed the "brain's best friend," extend an invitation to improved mood and emotional resilience. For those pursuing a plant-based path, flaxseeds and chia seeds offer plant-derived omega-3s, presenting a bridge between dietary preferences and brain health.

2. Complex Carbohydrates: Sustained Energy, Elevated Mood

Whole grains, like oats, quinoa, and brown rice, form the bedrock of sustained energy and mood stability. Carbohydrates, often unfairly maligned, serve as precursors to serotonin production—a neurotransmitter renowned for its "feel-good" effects. By ushering in steady energy release and harmonizing mood swings, complex carbohydrates assume their rightful role as architects of emotional balance.

3. Lean Protein: The Building Blocks of Emotional Resilience

Lean protein sources, spanning lean meats, poultry, eggs, and legumes, wield an arsenal of amino acids essential for the synthesis of neurotransmitters like dopamine and serotonin. These biochemical messengers orchestrate mood regulation and emotional harmony. Through the assimilation of adequate protein, you lay the foundation for the creation of these mood-enhancing chemicals.

4. Antioxidant-Rich Foods: Guardians of Brain Health

A kaleidoscope of colorful fruits and vegetables—berries, citrus fruits, leafy greens, and bell peppers—unites under the banner of antioxidants. These protective compounds shield brain cells from oxidative stress, nurturing cognitive function and emotional well-being. The symphony of colors on your plate becomes an ode to brain health and positive mood.

5. Gut-Healthy Foods: The Microbial Maestros of Mood

Fermented wonders like yogurt, kefir, sauerkraut, and kimchi usher in a host of beneficial probiotics to the gut, heralding a harmonious gut microbiome. The gut-brain connection dances to the tune of a balanced microbial community, translating into improved mood regulation and mitigation of anxiety and depression symptoms.

6. Nuts and Seeds: The Nutrient-Rich Emissaries of Emotional Wellness

Nuts and seeds—almonds, walnuts, pumpkin seeds—stand as emissaries of a nutrient-rich kingdom. Omega-3 fatty acids, antioxidants, and magnesium are their precious offerings. The stage they set is one of brain nourishment and emotional well-being.

7. Dark Chocolate: Decadence Meets Neurochemistry

Dark chocolate, often indulged in with delight, boasts compounds that spark the release of endorphins—the natural elixirs of pleasure and happiness. Wrapped in antioxidants, dark chocolate not only lifts the spirits but also nurtures brain health.

8. Herbal Teas: Steeped Serenity and Calm

Herbal teas—chamomile, lavender, peppermint—unveil their enchanting properties, weaving a tapestry of serenity and calm. These brews extend a calming hand, reducing stress and anxiety. Sipping on these teas becomes a ritual of self-soothing and emotional rejuvenation.

9. Water and Hydration: The Fountain of Cognitive Balance

The simplicity of water, often overlooked, is pivotal in maintaining cognitive function and emotional stability. Dehydration, a silent adversary, casts shadows of irritability, fatigue, and diminished focus. Sipping water throughout the day emerges as a fundamental pillar of overall well-being, including mood modulation.

10. Mindful Eating Practices: The Art of Present Consumption

In the midst of tangible foods, the concept of mindful eating emerges as a transformative practice. Mindfulness, applied to eating, invites a heightened awareness of each bite, each flavor, and each texture. Savored in the absence of distraction, meals become anchors of intentionality—a practice that nurtures a positive and profound connection with nourishment.

11. Leafy Greens and B Vitamins: Verdant Vitality for the Mind

Leafy greens, ranging from spinach to kale, are verdant powerhouses rich in B vitamins, including folate and B6. These vitamins play a pivotal role in mood regulation and neurotransmitter synthesis. Folate, in particular, supports the production of serotonin, promoting a sense of well-being and emotional stability. Incorporating these greens into your meals offers a burst of vitality that extends beyond physical health, nurturing your mental and emotional landscape.

12. Colorful Bell Peppers: Capsaicin and Endorphin Dance

The vibrant array of bell peppers brings not only a visual delight but also a mood-boosting compound—capsaicin. Capsaicin triggers the release of endorphins, those wondrous natural painkillers that also induce feelings of pleasure and euphoria. As you savor the spectrum of bell pepper hues, you're igniting an endorphin dance that elevates your mood and adds a touch of spicy delight to your emotional well-being.

13. Oysters and Zinc: A Zinc-Laden Elixir of Positivity

Oysters, often celebrated as aphrodisiacs, hold a treasure trove of zinc—a mineral closely linked to mood regulation and cognitive function. Zinc deficiency has been associated with depressive symptoms, making these shellfish an unexpected elixir of positivity. As you indulge in oysters, you're not only savoring their briny essence but also fortifying your emotional resilience through the power of essential minerals.

14. Probiotic-Rich Kombucha: Bubbling Fermentation of Joy

Kombucha, the effervescent elixir born of fermentation, contains probiotics that support gut health and, in turn, emotional balance. A flourishing gut microbiome is a haven for neurotransmitter production and mood modulation. With each sip of kombucha, you're infusing your system with microbial allies that dance harmoniously with your emotional landscape.

15. Vibrant Berries: Anthocyanins and Cognitive Cheer

The symphony of berries—blueberries, strawberries, raspberries—offers a palette of anthocyanin-rich hues. These flavonoids not only provide a burst of antioxidants for brain protection but also promote cognitive function and memory retention. The vibrant flavors of berries resonate with the joy of summer days, infusing your emotional terrain with a touch of cognitive cheer.

A Plate of Emotional Resilience

As you weave together the varied threads of these mood-enhancing foods, you're creating a plate that resonates with emotional resilience. The synergy of these nutrients, carefully selected and harmoniously consumed, is akin to an orchestra tuning its instruments for a soul-stirring performance. In the crescendo of each bite, you're supporting neurotransmitter production, reducing inflammation, and fostering a positive emotional terrain.

The Journey Beyond the Plate

Chapter 11 isn't just a guide to selecting foods; it's a testament to the transformational potential of conscious consumption. Beyond the culinary symphony, it emphasizes the art of mindful connection—to ingredients, to flavors, and ultimately, to yourself. As you heed the wisdom of these foods, you embark on a journey that transcends mere sustenance. You're crafting a lifestyle that celebrates the interplay between nutrition and emotional well-being—a symphony of nourishment that resonates far beyond the plate and deep within your soul.

Elevate Your Plate, Elevate Your Mood
As you embark on the journey of curating a mood-boosting plate, remember that no single food is a magic solution for mental wellness. Rather, it's the synergy of a balanced and varied diet that supports your brain health and emotional equilibrium. The foods listed in this chapter offer a blueprint for creating meals that nourish both your body and mind. By incorporating a wide array of nutrient-dense foods, you're providing your brain with the tools it needs to regulate mood, manage stress, and foster emotional resilience.

The Mindful Connection
Pairing your food choices with mindful eating practices amplifies their impact on your emotional well-being. Mindful eating encourages you to slow down, savor each bite, and cultivate gratitude for the nourishment your meal provides. This practice enhances your awareness of the effects that food has on your body and mood, allowing you to make conscious choices that align with your well-being goals.

A Holistic Approach to Mental Wellness

Chapter 11 transcends the idea of food as a means of physical sustenance and positions it as an essential component of a holistic approach to mental wellness. By selecting foods that support brain health, stabilize mood, and promote emotional resilience, you're taking a proactive step toward nurturing your mind and spirit.

Chapter 12: Navigating Dining Out and Social Eating

In the modern world, eating extends beyond the boundaries of our personal kitchens. It's a social activity that often takes place in restaurants, cafes, parties, and gatherings. Chapter 12, "Navigating Dining Out and Social Eating," is a compass that guides you through the complexities of social eating while staying aligned with your mental wellness goals. This chapter is your toolkit for practicing mindful eating, fostering positive relationships with food, and maintaining your nourished journey in the face of diverse culinary landscapes.

The Social Tapestry of Eating

In the intricate fabric of human existence, few elements are as deeply intertwined with our emotional, cultural, and social experiences as eating. Food is more than mere sustenance; it serves as a conduit for connections, a vessel for traditions, and a means to celebrate life's moments. The concept of "The Social Tapestry of Eating," as explored in Chapter 12, delves into the profound role that dining together plays in our lives, highlighting its significance in building relationships, preserving cultural heritage, and fostering communal bonds.

A Feast of Shared Experiences

At its core, eating is a communal act—an opportunity to come together, share stories, and build relationships. Throughout history, cultures have gathered around meals to connect, exchange ideas, and strengthen bonds. From the family dinner table to grand feasts celebrating milestones, food serves as a medium through which we communicate love, friendship, and camaraderie.

Cultural Traditions and Culinary Heritage
The social tapestry of eating is intricately woven with threads of cultural traditions and culinary heritage. Each culture boasts a rich tapestry of dishes, recipes, and practices that reflect its history, values, and way of life. Culinary traditions are passed down from generation to generation, and sharing these traditional meals becomes a way to honor the past and celebrate the present. Be it a Thanksgiving feast, a Diwali celebration, or a Lunar New Year banquet, these culinary experiences anchor us to our roots and reinforce our sense of belonging.

Celebration and Joy
Food is often at the center of celebrations, from birthdays to weddings, holidays to festivals. These occasions are marked by the abundance of dishes, the laughter of loved ones, and the joy that accompanies shared moments. The act of feasting is not just about satisfying physical hunger; it's about celebrating life's milestones and expressing gratitude for the bonds that tie us together. Food becomes a tangible expression of joy and celebration, turning ordinary meals into extraordinary experiences.

Challenges of Social Eating

While the social tapestry of eating is rich and rewarding, it also presents challenges, particularly when it comes to aligning our nutritional goals with social scenarios. The abundance of options at restaurants, the allure of indulgent treats at parties, and the pressure to conform to social norms can all create tension between our wellness intentions and our actions. Striking a balance between participating in these shared experiences and staying true to our health goals requires a delicate dance—one that requires mindfulness and intentionality.

The Gift of Mindful Connection

Chapter 12 encourages us to embrace the social tapestry of eating as an opportunity for mindful connection—with food, with ourselves, and with others. It offers strategies for navigating diverse dining scenarios while honoring our wellness goals. By choosing to engage in mindful eating, we elevate our dining experiences beyond the superficial and transform them into moments of mindfulness, gratitude, and shared connection. Through these practices, we reinforce the bonds that tie us together and create a tapestry of well-being that extends to both our individual selves and the world around us.

Mindful Eating: Your Anchor in Social Scenarios

In a world brimming with distractions and rapid-fire experiences, the art of mindful eating emerges as a serene sanctuary—a haven of awareness that guides us through the labyrinthine landscape of social eating. Chapter 12 tenderly unveils the concept of mindful eating as a profound anchor, empowering us to navigate the often tumultuous waters of shared meals with grace, presence, and a profound connection to our well-being.

The Power of Mindful Eating

Mindful eating is a practice that transcends the act of consuming food. It's a holistic experience that invites us to be fully present in the moment, immersing ourselves in the textures, flavors, and sensations that accompany each bite. This practice strips away the automatic and mindless tendencies that can characterize our eating habits, ushering in a profound awareness that enriches our relationship with food and our own bodies.

Mindful Eating in Social Settings

Amid the chatter of social settings—restaurants bustling with activity, tables laden with delectable dishes, and the hum of conversation—mindful eating emerges as a guiding light, illuminating a path of intentionality in the midst of abundance. It allows us to remain anchored to our own wellness goals, even as we engage with the communal and celebratory aspects of shared meals.

Savoring Each Bite

Mindful eating encourages us to savor each bite as if it were a treasure to be cherished. In social scenarios, this practice offers a way to engage deeply with our meals, allowing us to fully appreciate the flavors, textures, and aromas that grace our plates. By savoring each bite, we cultivate an intimate connection with our food, turning the act of eating into a sensory celebration.

Honoring Hunger and Fullness

One of the cornerstones of mindful eating is attuning ourselves to our body's cues. In social settings, where external stimuli and social pressures can influence our eating choices, this skill becomes invaluable. Mindful eating empowers us to recognize true hunger and to gauge when we are comfortably satisfied. It allows us to bypass the tug of external cues and make choices that honor our body's needs.

Cultivating Connection in Conversation

Mindful eating doesn't isolate us from the social aspect of dining; rather, it enriches our interactions. Engaging in mindful conversation while savoring our meal creates a harmonious symphony of connection. We engage with others with authenticity and presence, while also engaging with ourselves through the act of nourishment. This symbiosis of connection amplifies the joy of shared meals, turning them into moments of meaningful interaction.

Mindful Eating as a Compass

In the landscape of social eating, mindful eating serves as a compass that points us towards choices aligned with our wellness intentions. It allows us to navigate menus with clarity, choose portions that resonate with our bodies, and participate in the social experience with a heightened sense of awareness. Mindful eating is a tool that empowers us to make conscious decisions, fostering harmony between our social engagements and our well-being.

A Transformative Practice

Chapter 12 invites us to recognize mindful eating as more than a technique—it's a transformative practice that fosters self-awareness, self-compassion, and a profound connection to our own bodies and emotions. Through the lens of mindful eating, social eating is transformed from a potential challenge into an opportunity for growth, presence, and nourishment on multiple levels. With each mindful bite, we are not only savoring the flavors of our meal but also cultivating a deeper relationship with ourselves and the world around us.

Strategies for Mindful Eating in Different Scenarios

1. Restaurants and Cafes:

Navigating restaurant menus can be a joyful yet overwhelming experience. Opt for dishes that align with your nutritional goals, and don't hesitate to ask for modifications to suit your preferences. Take your time to explore the flavors, textures, and aromas of your meal. Chew slowly, savoring each bite, and pause periodically to gauge your fullness level.

2. Parties and Gatherings:
Social gatherings often come with a plethora of tempting treats and indulgent options. Prior to attending, have a light, balanced snack to prevent arriving overly hungry. Survey the food offerings before loading your plate, and opt for smaller portions of your favorites. Engage in conversation and connect with others, allowing your eating pace to sync with the rhythm of the event.

3. Office Lunches:
Office lunches may involve communal meals or ordering takeout. Plan ahead by packing a balanced lunch or choosing nourishing options from the menu. Engage in mindful eating by stepping away from your desk and finding a quiet space to enjoy your meal. Focus on the sensory experience and give yourself permission to take breaks and refuel.

4. Celebratory Occasions:
Holidays and special occasions often feature traditional foods and family recipes. Approach these occasions with a flexible mindset, allowing yourself to savor the dishes without guilt. Balance indulgence with mindful choices, such as prioritizing vegetables and lean proteins. Engage in conversations and create lasting memories while being present in the moment.

5. Travel and New Culinary Experiences:

Exploring new cuisines during travel can be a delightful adventure. Research local dishes that align with your nutritional preferences. Embrace the experience of trying new foods mindfully, paying attention to flavors and textures. If portions are large, consider sharing dishes with others to avoid overeating.

Cultivating Mindful Presence
Mindful eating extends beyond food selection; it encompasses cultivating a sense of presence and awareness in every eating scenario. Set intentions before each meal to eat with mindfulness, irrespective of the setting. Use the STOP technique: Stop, Take a Breath, Observe your thoughts and feelings, and Proceed with intention. This practice grounds you, allowing you to make conscious choices aligned with your mental well-being.

Transforming Social Eating into Nourishing Moments
Chapter 12 is an invitation to view social eating not as a challenge but as an opportunity to foster mindful connections with food and people. By practicing mindful eating techniques, you're infusing intentionality into each bite, turning ordinary meals into nourishing moments. Your journey of wellness isn't about isolation; it's about navigating the social tapestry with grace and authenticity. With every shared meal, you have the power to create an experience that honors both your mental well-being and the joy of human connection.

Chapter 13: Sustaining Your Progress

Chapter 13 marks a pivotal juncture in your journey toward sustained mental wellness. It's a guidepost that illuminates the path to maintaining and building upon the progress you've achieved by incorporating mindful eating and nourishment into your lifestyle. This chapter serves as a compass, steering you through the challenges that may arise and offer strategies to ensure that your improved mental health is not just a fleeting moment but a steadfast foundation for a flourishing life.

The Continuum of Wellness

As you stand at the crossroads of sustained progress, it's crucial to recognize that wellness is not an endpoint; it's a continuous journey. Chapter 13 reiterates the concept of mental wellness as a dynamic continuum—a journey marked by ebbs and flows, victories and setbacks. Armed with the knowledge you've acquired, you're prepared to traverse this continuum with resilience and determination.

Cultivating Lasting Nutritional Habits

Building upon the mindful eating practices you've embraced, this chapter delves into the art of cultivating lasting nutritional habits. It's about transforming these practices from intentional efforts into inherent behaviors— nourishing habits that seamlessly integrate with your daily life. Through consistent, conscious choices, you fortify your foundation of well-being, ensuring that your nutritional choices remain aligned with your mental health goals.

Creating an Environment for Success

The environment in which you exist plays a significant role in sustaining progress. Chapter 13 sheds light on crafting an environment that nurtures your mental wellness aspirations. This includes stocking your kitchen with nourishing ingredients, having go-to recipes for quick and healthy meals, and fostering a supportive social network that celebrates your journey. A supportive environment serves as a cocoon of positivity, shielding you from potential triggers and setbacks.

Mindful Decision-Making

Sustaining progress hinges on the power of mindful decision-making. This chapter equips you with strategies to make thoughtful choices, even in the face of challenges. Whether it's navigating a menu at a restaurant, resisting emotional eating triggers, or staying attuned to hunger and fullness cues, mindfulness is your steadfast companion. By consistently making choices aligned with your wellness goals, you're forging a resilient path forward.

Self-Compassion and Adaptability

In the pursuit of sustained progress, self-compassion becomes your guiding light. Acknowledge that setbacks are a natural part of the journey, and treat yourself with kindness and understanding. This chapter underscores the importance of adaptability, encouraging you to learn from challenges rather than succumb to them. Embrace flexibility as you navigate unexpected twists, understanding that adaptability is a cornerstone of lasting growth.

The Role of Professional Guidance

Recognizing when to seek professional guidance is a hallmark of wisdom and self-care. This chapter acknowledges the significance of collaboration with healthcare providers, nutritionists, and mental health experts. They offer tailored guidance, monitoring, and support to ensure that your journey toward sustained mental wellness remains anchored in evidence-based practices.

Leveraging Progress for Further Growth

Sustaining progress is not just about maintaining the status quo—it's about leveraging your achievements for further growth. This chapter delves into expanding your horizons by exploring new foods, recipes, and wellness practices. By continuously enriching your understanding of the symbiotic relationship between nutrition and mental health, you're poised to embrace a life of ongoing discovery and empowerment.

Cultivating a Legacy of Wellness: A Journey Forward

As you immerse yourself in the pages of Chapter 13, you are embarking on a journey that extends far beyond the bounds of a single chapter. This chapter is a cornerstone—a bridge connecting the progress you've made to the limitless possibilities that lie ahead. It's a continuation of the narrative you've been crafting—the story of your transformation, resilience, and unwavering commitment to your own well-being.

Harnessing the Power of Reflection
Chapter 13 encourages you to embrace the power of reflection. Take moments to pause and acknowledge the distance you've traveled. Recall the challenges you've surmounted, the victories you've celebrated, and the lessons you've learned along the way. Reflect on the impact that mindful eating and conscious nutrition have had on your mental wellness. Through reflection, you gain perspective, anchoring yourself in the present while honoring the strides you've made.

The Ripples of Inspiration
Your journey of sustained progress becomes a beacon of inspiration—a source of illumination for those around you. As you embody the principles of mindful eating and holistic nourishment, your actions serve as a testament to the transformational power of intentional choices. Your friends, family, and peers witness your evolution and draw inspiration from your dedication. Your journey isn't just personal; it radiates outward, encouraging others to embark on their own quests for wellness.

Fostering Empowerment Through Knowledge

The wisdom you've accumulated throughout your journey is a gift—one that empowers you and those you touch with a profound understanding of the synergy between nutrition and mental wellness. This chapter empowers you to wield this knowledge as a tool for advocacy and education. Share your insights, experiences, and discoveries with others. Become a catalyst for change, sparking conversations that raise awareness about the vital connection between nourishment and emotional equilibrium.

Evolution: The Key to Enduring Progress
In the realm of sustained progress, evolution is your steadfast ally. This chapter invites you to embrace the ever-evolving nature of your journey. As you continue to explore new foods, adapt your habits, and deepen your understanding, you're perpetuating a cycle of growth. The essence of progress lies not just in maintaining what you've achieved but also in continually expanding your horizons, pushing boundaries, and redefining what's possible.

A Legacy Beyond Yourself
Your journey is a legacy—an offering that extends beyond your personal sphere. By embracing sustained progress and wellness, you're contributing to a paradigm shift—a movement that redefines our relationship with nourishment, mindfulness, and mental health. Your legacy encompasses a world where individuals recognize the power they hold to shape their well-being through their choices. It's a world

where conversations around nutrition become conversations about empowerment, self-care, and vitality.

A Future Illuminated by Wellness

As you navigate the rich terrain of Chapter 13, envision the future you're forging—a future illuminated by wellness, resilience, and holistic balance. With every mindful bite, every choice that aligns with your well-being, you're sowing the seeds of a vibrant existence. You're crafting a narrative that isn't just about the destination but about the transformative journey itself. This journey is marked by progress, reflection, inspiration, empowerment, evolution, and a legacy that transcends time.

Continuing the Story

As you continue your exploration of Chapter 13, remember that you are part of a timeless narrative—a narrative of well-being, growth, and transformation. The progress you've sustained is a testament to your dedication and your belief in the profound connection between what you nourish your body with and the vitality of your mind and spirit. As you close this chapter, know that the story is far from over. It's a story that will continue to unfold, guided by the principles you've embraced, the wisdom you've gained, and the legacy you're creating—a legacy that illuminates the path for others and leaves an indelible mark on the world.

Chapter 14: When to Seek Professional Help

Chapter 14 stands as a beacon of insight and guidance, illuminating the critical juncture where individual efforts intersect with professional expertise. This chapter delves into the delicate balance between personal empowerment and the recognition that seeking professional help is an act of self-care and wisdom. It is a profound exploration of the signs, nuances, and circumstances that signal the need for collaboration with healthcare providers—a testament to the comprehensive approach to mental wellness that goes beyond self-reliance.

The Intersection of Empowerment and Professional Insight

In the journey of enhancing mental wellness through nutrition, empowerment has been a cornerstone. The practices of mindful eating, nurturing nutritional habits, and fostering a harmonious relationship with food are emblematic of taking ownership of one's well-being. Chapter 14 continues this narrative by introducing the concept of seeking professional help not as a relinquishment of control, but as an extension of self-empowerment. It acknowledges that recognizing the need for guidance is an act of wisdom, highlighting that even the most self-aware individuals can benefit from the expertise of trained professionals.

Navigating the Complex Terrain of Mental Wellness

Mental wellness is a complex tapestry woven from myriad threads—genetics, environment, lifestyle, and nutrition. While nutrition plays a vital role, it's essential to acknowledge that it's just one aspect of the holistic puzzle. Chapter 14 delves into the understanding that certain conditions and challenges may necessitate a multifaceted approach, involving collaboration with healthcare providers who specialize in mental health, psychology, and medical care.

Recognizing the Signs: When to Collaborate
This chapter provides invaluable insights into recognizing the signs that indicate the need for professional help. It addresses situations where the challenges may extend beyond the realm of nutrition, including severe mood disorders, persistent anxiety, depression, eating disorders, and other mental health conditions. It underscores the importance of not only paying attention to your body's cues but also acknowledging shifts in your emotional landscape. By attuning yourself to emotional imbalances and persistent challenges, you empower yourself to make informed decisions about seeking professional guidance.

Holistic Assessment and Tailored Strategies
Collaboration with healthcare providers offers the advantage of a comprehensive assessment. It involves evaluating physical health, mental well-being, medical history, and potential underlying factors. This chapter emphasizes the tailored strategies that professionals can provide, taking into account your unique circumstances and

needs. Whether it's designing a personalized nutrition plan, suggesting therapy, or prescribing medication when appropriate, professionals bring a wealth of specialized knowledge to the table.

The Courage to Reach Out

Acknowledging the need for professional help requires courage and vulnerability. This chapter acknowledges that taking this step isn't a sign of weakness but a testament to your commitment to your well-being. It addresses the common fears and stigmas associated with seeking help and empowers you to transcend these barriers. It reassures you that reaching out for professional guidance is an act of self-love and strength—a conscious choice that reflects your determination to live a life of optimal mental health.

Fostering a Collaborative Partnership

Collaboration with healthcare providers is not a one-way street—it's a partnership. This chapter highlights the importance of open communication, transparency, and active participation in your care. Professionals value your insights, experiences, and preferences as integral components of crafting a comprehensive treatment plan. Your input enriches the collaborative process and ensures that the strategies devised align with your unique journey.

Breaking Down the Myths and Misconceptions

Chapter 14 confronts the myths and misconceptions that often shroud the concept of seeking professional help. It dispels the notion that it's solely for severe cases or moments of crisis, highlighting that early intervention can prevent challenges from escalating. It also addresses the notion that seeking help negates personal efforts—it's quite the opposite. Collaboration amplifies your efforts, providing you with tools, insights, and support to enhance your well-being journey.

The Ripple Effect of Professional Help
By embracing the wisdom of seeking professional help, you're not only nurturing your own mental health but also influencing a broader sphere. This chapter touches upon the ripple effect—how your actions inspire others to prioritize their well-being and destigmatize seeking help. As you normalize this act, you contribute to a cultural shift—one where individuals recognize that reaching out for guidance is a courageous step toward living a life of holistic wellness.

Elevating Your Well-Being Through Collaboration
Chapter 14 is a chapter that resonates with the spirit of growth, evolution, and the pursuit of well-being. It beckons you to step beyond the bounds of self-sufficiency and embrace the transformative potential of collaboration. Your journey has brought you to a crossroads—a juncture where the synergy of personal efforts and professional insight can propel you toward greater heights of mental wellness.

Embracing the Holistic Approach

Mental wellness is a mosaic woven from diverse elements—nutrition, psychology, medical care, and lifestyle. Chapter 14 underscores the holistic nature of mental well-being by urging you to consider a multidimensional approach. It acknowledges that while nutrition is a powerful tool, there are instances where the tapestry of your challenges may be woven with threads that extend beyond food. Collaboration with professionals brings these threads into focus, allowing for a comprehensive understanding of your well-being.

The Wisdom of Seeking Professional Help
This chapter reinforces the wisdom of recognizing your own limits and seeking professional help when needed. It's a testament to your understanding that the path to wellness isn't solitary, but one that can be enriched through the expertise of professionals. Whether you're grappling with persistent anxiety, overwhelming depression, or navigating complex emotional landscapes, reaching out for guidance is a stride of empowerment. It showcases your commitment to a life lived in alignment with your highest potential.

Navigating the Path to Collaboration
The process of seeking professional help is often shrouded in uncertainty and questions. Chapter 14 guides you through this journey with clarity and compassion. It offers insights on how to find the right healthcare providers, specialists, and therapists who align with your needs and values. It

sheds light on the art of forging a collaborative partnership—a relationship built on mutual respect, trust, and shared goals. As you embark on this path, remember that your voice and experiences are integral to this partnership, contributing to a tailored approach to your well-being.

Transformative Potential: From Challenges to Growth
Collaboration with healthcare providers is more than a response to challenges; it's a gateway to growth. This chapter underscores the transformative potential embedded within seeking professional help. It's an invitation to evolve, to understand yourself on a deeper level, and to acquire tools that empower you to navigate life's complexities. The insights gained through collaboration can catalyze profound shifts, leading to enhanced self-awareness, coping strategies, and a strengthened foundation of well-being.

Deconstructing Stigmas: Empowering a Culture of Care
Chapter 14 boldly addresses the stigmas and misconceptions that can cast shadows on the act of seeking professional help. It dismantles the notion that seeking assistance is a sign of weakness, emphasizing that it's an emblem of strength and self-awareness. By dispelling these myths, you're contributing to a cultural shift—one where conversations about mental health and seeking help are welcomed and normalized. Your decision to collaborate becomes an act of advocacy, fostering a culture of care and understanding.

A Tapestry of Transformation

In weaving together the threads of your personal efforts and the expertise of professionals, you're crafting a tapestry of transformation. Chapter 14 encapsulates this beautiful union—a testament to your journey's intricate interplay of self-discovery and professional insight. It's a chapter that celebrates the harmonious symphony of empowerment and collaboration—a narrative that unfolds with authenticity and authenticity.

Your Ongoing Journey

As you continue your exploration of Chapter 14, embrace the empowerment that comes with recognizing the value of professional guidance. Your journey is marked by self-discovery, resilience, and the courage to seek help when needed. It's a journey that demonstrates your commitment to mental wellness—an ongoing quest that evolves with each step. This chapter serves as a guiding light, illuminating the path to enriched well-being through collaboration—a path that is unique to you, filled with promise, growth, and a deeper understanding of yourself.

Chapter 15: Cultivating Long-Term Nutritional Habits

In the landscape of holistic well-being, Chapter 15 emerges as a cornerstone—a chapter dedicated to the art of sustainability and integration. It's a chapter that transcends the boundaries of short-term practices and delves into the realm of enduring transformation. Here, the principles of mental health-conscious eating cease to be a temporary endeavor and become an intrinsic part of your ongoing lifestyle. This chapter is your guide to weaving these principles into the very fabric of your existence, cultivating long-term nutritional habits that nourish both body and spirit.

The Evolution of Habits: Beyond the Six Weeks

As you embark on the journey of Chapter 15, it's crucial to embrace the reality that habits evolve over time. The six-week path you've traversed was a foundation—a crucible that kindled the fire of mindful eating and well-being. However, true transformation lies not in the completion of a predetermined timeframe, but in the continuation of the practices you've cultivated. This chapter invites you to transcend the notion of a finish line and recognize that your journey is perpetual, marked by growth, adaptation, and the gradual integration of mindful practices.

From Practice to Lifestyle: The Integration Process

Integration is an art—an intricate dance that involves seamlessly merging mindful eating practices into your daily routine. Chapter 15 guides you through this process, offering insights on how to infuse the essence of mental health-conscious eating into various aspects of your life. Whether it's meal planning, grocery shopping, dining out, or celebrating special occasions, this chapter empowers you to navigate diverse scenarios while upholding your commitment to well-being.

Mindful Meal Planning: A Blueprint for Success
Meal planning isn't just a tactical approach to eating—it's a reflection of your commitment to your well-being. This chapter delves into the practice of mindful meal planning, offering strategies to create balanced, nourishing meals that resonate with your nutritional goals. It invites you to embrace diversity, incorporate seasonal produce, and explore new recipes that align with your holistic approach to health.

Navigating Social Scenarios: The Mindful Diner
Eating is often a social experience—a tapestry woven with shared moments and connections. Chapter 15 recognizes the significance of dining out and social eating, offering guidance on how to stay aligned with your values while embracing the joy of communal meals. Whether it's practicing mindfulness while ordering, seeking out health-conscious options, or gracefully navigating social pressures, this chapter equips you to honor your well-being in a variety of contexts.

Embracing Flexibility and Adaptability

The journey of integration is not without its twists and turns. This chapter acknowledges that life is dynamic, and there will be moments when your well-laid plans may need to be adjusted. It encourages you to embrace flexibility and adaptability—traits that are essential for cultivating sustainable habits. Whether it's unexpected events, changes in routine, or moments of indulgence, your ability to navigate these situations while staying anchored in your principles is a testament to your growth.

Nurturing Intuitive Eating: The Inner Guide

Intuitive eating is a hallmark of long-term well-being—a practice that goes beyond rigid rules and embraces attunement to your body's signals. This chapter delves into the art of intuitive eating, empowering you to listen to your body, honor hunger and fullness cues, and make choices that resonate with your well-being. It's about rekindling the connection between body and mind, allowing your inner guide to lead the way.

Rituals of Self-Care: A Nurturing Routine

As you integrate mindful practices into your lifestyle, rituals of self-care become essential cornerstones. This chapter explores the concept of rituals—moments of intentional nourishment that extend beyond food. Whether it's engaging in mindful movement, practicing meditation, or cultivating gratitude, these rituals contribute to your overall sense of well-being, enriching your journey with moments of joy, serenity, and self-reflection.

The Legacy of Integration: A Lifestyle Transformed
Chapter 15 isn't just about integration—it's about legacy. By cultivating long-term nutritional habits, you're leaving an imprint—a legacy of well-being that resonates through time. The practices you've embraced become woven into the tapestry of your existence, shaping the narrative of your life. Your journey transcends individual moments and emerges as a profound transformation—a transformation that extends beyond you, touching the lives of those around you and inspiring a culture of holistic well-being.

Honoring Your Journey of Transformation
Chapter 15 is a chapter of celebration—a celebration of your journey of transformation and the evolution of your relationship with food and well-being. It acknowledges the profound shift that has taken place within you—a shift from fleeting practices to lasting habits, from external rules to intuitive choices. This chapter is a testament to your commitment to holistic health and your willingness to embrace the ongoing path of growth.

The Dance of Integration

Integration is a dance—a dance that harmonizes the rhythms of mindful eating with the melodies of your daily life. This chapter explores the graceful choreography of integrating mindful practices into your routines, rituals, and choices. It emphasizes the value of consistency, not rigidity, as you merge mindfulness with your actions. Whether it's savoring the flavors of your meals, staying present during a conversation, or choosing foods that honor your well-being, integration is about weaving mindfulness into the fabric of each moment.

Thriving Amidst Diversity: Tailoring Your Approach
Just as every individual is unique, so too is the journey of integration. This chapter encourages you to tailor your approach to suit your individual needs and circumstances. It acknowledges that the path to sustained well-being is marked by diversity—diverse foods, practices, and experiences. It's a reminder that your journey is dynamic, and what works for you may evolve over time. By embracing flexibility, you're cultivating resilience—an essential trait for navigating life's ebb and flow.

Navigating Challenges: An Opportunity for Growth
Integration is not without its challenges. It's a voyage marked by learning curves, moments of uncertainty, and the occasional detour. This chapter reframes challenges as opportunities for growth—lessons that deepen your understanding of yourself and your well-being. Whether it's a setback in your routine, an unexpected craving, or a lapse

in mindfulness, each challenge becomes a stepping stone toward greater self-awareness and resilience.

Cultivating Self-Compassion: Your Steadfast Guide

The journey of integration invites you to be gentle with yourself—to embrace self-compassion as a guiding light. This chapter underscores the importance of self-compassion, especially during moments of imperfection. It's a reminder that setbacks are not failures, but integral parts of the journey. By cultivating self-compassion, you're fostering a nurturing environment that supports your ongoing growth and evolution.

Mindful Movement: Nurturing Body and Soul

While Chapter 15 focuses on the integration of mindful eating, it also acknowledges the role of movement in holistic well-being. Engaging in mindful movement—whether it's yoga, walking, or other forms of exercise—can be a powerful complement to your nutritional habits. Movement not only supports physical health but also enhances mood, reduces stress, and fosters a deeper mind-body connection.

Cultivating Gratitude and Reflection: The Art of Pause

Integration invites you to pause—to reflect on your journey, express gratitude for your progress, and set intentions for the road ahead. This chapter introduces practices of gratitude and reflection as integral components of your ongoing path. By savoring your accomplishments, acknowledging your growth, and envisioning your aspirations, you're cultivating a mindset of positivity and empowerment.

The Ripple Effect: A Gift to Yourself and Others

As you immerse yourself in the wisdom of Chapter 15, remember that your journey has a ripple effect—a profound impact that extends beyond your own well-being. By embracing mindful practices and cultivating long-term nutritional habits, you're contributing to a culture of holistic health. Your choices inspire others to consider their own well-being, fostering a collective movement toward wellness and self-care.

Embracing the Infinite Journey

In closing, Chapter 15 encourages you to embrace the infinite journey of well-being—a journey that doesn't have a destination but is marked by continuous growth and self-discovery. The principles of mental health-conscious eating have become a part of you, guiding your choices, enriching your experiences, and nurturing your soul. As you turn the pages of this chapter, recognize that you're not concluding a process; rather, you're stepping onto a path illuminated by your own empowerment and the unwavering commitment to a life lived in harmony with your deepest values.

Chapter 16: Beyond Food - Movement, Mindfulness, and Joy

In the symphony of well-being, Chapter 16 introduces harmonious melodies that go beyond the realm of nutrition. This chapter is an exploration of the interconnectedness between the mind, body, and spirit—a journey that encompasses movement, mindfulness, and the pursuit of joy. It delves into the profound impact these practices have on your mental health, unveiling the transformative potential that arises when they are woven into the fabric of your holistic approach to well-being.

The Dynamic Duo: Nutrition and Complementary Practices

As you venture into Chapter 16, it's essential to recognize that nutrition is not the sole instrument in the orchestra of well-being. It's one element of a symphony that includes movement, mindfulness, and cultivating joy. This chapter elucidates the synergy between these practices, acknowledging that they are threads that can be woven together to create a tapestry of enhanced mental wellness.

The Power of Movement: Nurturing Mind and Body

Movement is a celebration of the body—a dance of vitality that nurtures both physical and mental well-being. This chapter sheds light on the transformative power of movement, whether it's through yoga, jogging, dancing, or any form of exercise that resonates with you. Movement has been linked to improved mood, reduced stress, enhanced cognitive function, and increased self-esteem. It's an invitation to honor your body's capacity for strength, flexibility, and resilience—a journey that contributes to a positive relationship with your physical self.

The Art of Mindfulness: Cultivating Present-Moment Awareness

Mindfulness is a cornerstone of well-being—a practice that invites you to be fully present in each moment without judgment. Chapter 16 delves into the practice of mindfulness, offering insights into meditation, deep breathing, and mindfulness techniques that foster emotional regulation and stress reduction. Mindfulness enhances self-awareness, helps manage intrusive thoughts, and fosters a sense of calm amidst life's fluctuations. By weaving mindfulness into your daily routine, you're cultivating a mental sanctuary—a space of stillness and clarity.

Pursuing Joy: A Path to Emotional Resilience

Joy is a beacon—a light that illuminates the path to emotional resilience. This chapter embraces the pursuit of joy as an integral part of mental wellness. Engaging in activities that bring joy—whether it's pursuing hobbies, spending time with loved ones, or connecting with nature—can elevate your mood, increase positive emotions, and create a buffer against stress and challenges. This pursuit of joy is a reminder that well-being is not solely about managing difficulties, but also about embracing the moments that bring delight and fulfillment.

Integration in Action: A Holistic Practice

Chapter 16 isn't about compartmentalization—it's about integration. It's about infusing the principles of movement, mindfulness, and joy into your daily life in ways that resonate with your unique journey. This chapter offers practical strategies to seamlessly incorporate these practices into your routines—whether it's taking mindful pauses during your day, engaging in movement breaks, or intentionally seeking moments of joy. It's an embodiment of holistic well-being—a symphony in which every note contributes to the melody of mental wellness.

The Balance of Time and Space

In your exploration of Chapter 16, it's important to honor the balance of time and space. While these practices offer transformative benefits, they also require a commitment to consistency and patience. This chapter encourages you to create a dedicated space in your life for movement, mindfulness, and joy. It's a reminder that self-care is not a luxury, but an essential investment in your mental health.

A Journey of Self-Discovery and Transformation

Chapter 16 encapsulates a journey—an expedition of self-discovery and transformation. It beckons you to explore the realms beyond nutrition, inviting you to venture into the landscapes of movement, mindfulness, and joy. This chapter is a testament to the dynamic interplay between these practices, their profound influence on your mental well-being, and the collective impact they have when integrated into your holistic approach to life.

Movement: A Dance of Liberation
Movement is more than physical activity—it's a dance of liberation for both the body and the mind. This chapter delves into the intricate tapestry of movement, inviting you to embrace the joy of bodily expression. Whether it's the meditative flow of yoga, the invigoration of a morning jog, or the release of tension through dance, movement has the power to elevate your mood, boost endorphins, and foster a sense of accomplishment. By engaging in movement, you're not only caring for your physical health but also nurturing your emotional well-being.

Mindfulness: The Gateway to Inner Harmony
Mindfulness is a practice that bridges the gap between the outer world and your inner sanctuary. Chapter 16 delves into the art of mindfulness—a journey of cultivating presence, awareness, and acceptance. Mindfulness allows you to detach from the chaos of daily life and immerse yourself in the richness of the present moment. It's a practice that promotes emotional regulation, reduces rumination, and enhances self-compassion. By weaving

mindfulness into your routines, you're fostering a deeper connection with yourself and the world around you.

The Quest for Joy: Fueling Resilience

Joy is a currency of well-being—a treasure that enriches your emotional bank. This chapter celebrates the pursuit of joy as an essential component of mental wellness. It encourages you to prioritize activities that ignite your passion, whether it's reading, painting, playing a musical instrument, or simply spending time with loved ones. The pursuit of joy is not a luxury; it's a necessity that contributes to emotional resilience, stress reduction, and an overall positive outlook on life.

Synchronicity of Practices: Amplifying Well-Being

Chapter 16 unfolds as a symphony—a composition of movement, mindfulness, and joy harmonizing to amplify your well-being. These practices are not isolated, but interconnected, weaving together to create a holistic tapestry of health. The synergy between these practices is a reminder that your journey of well-being is multifaceted, and each practice enriches the others. Engaging in movement can deepen your mindfulness practice, and finding joy can enhance the benefits of both movement and mindfulness.

A Living Canvas: Your Holistic Lifestyle

In your exploration of Chapter 16, envision your life as a canvas—a canvas upon which movement, mindfulness, and joy are painted with vibrant strokes. These practices are the hues that infuse your life with depth, meaning, and vitality. This chapter empowers you to embrace these practices as an integral part of your holistic lifestyle—a lifestyle that resonates with authenticity, empowerment, and a commitment to nurturing your mental health.

Cultivating a Resilient Mind-Body Connection

Chapter 16 unfolds as a sanctuary—a haven where the wisdom of movement, mindfulness, and joy converges to cultivate a resilient mind-body connection. It beckons you to recognize the profound interplay between these practices, each a thread contributing to the tapestry of your mental well-being. This chapter isn't just about activities; it's about the mindful cultivation of a life imbued with intention, awareness, and positivity.

Movement as Embodiment

Movement is an embodiment—an expression of the vitality within you. This chapter delves into the essence of movement, inviting you to honor your body's ability to stretch, strengthen, and thrive. Whether it's the graceful flow of tai chi, the groundedness of Pilates, or the exhilaration of hiking, movement is a celebration of your physical self. It stimulates the release of endorphins, the brain's natural mood enhancers, and establishes a harmonious connection between your body's rhythm and your mental state.

Mindfulness: A Sanctuary Within

Mindfulness is a sanctuary—a sacred space where you can find solace amidst life's turbulence. This chapter delves into the sanctuary of mindfulness, offering insights into meditation, breathwork, and mindfulness practices that anchor you to the present moment. Mindfulness reshapes your relationship with thoughts and emotions, empowering you to observe them without judgment. By integrating mindfulness into your days, you're fostering emotional regulation, reducing stress, and nurturing a compassionate connection with yourself.

The Joy Quest: Cultivating Positive Emotions

Joy is an elixir—a potion of positive emotions that elevates your mental landscape. This chapter extols the pursuit of joy as a pathway to emotional well-being. It encourages you to engage in activities that spark delight, whether it's playing with pets, immersing in creative pursuits, or relishing moments of laughter with friends. Pursuing joy generates feelings of happiness, contentment, and gratitude, which, in turn, act as shields against stress and anxiety, nurturing your mental resilience.

The Interplay: A Holistic Choreography

Chapter 16 orchestrates a holistic choreography—an interplay where movement, mindfulness, and joy dance together in harmonious rhythm. These practices don't exist in isolation; they coalesce to amplify their impact on your well-being. Movement nurtures a sense of groundedness that complements the mindfulness journey. Mindfulness, in turn, enhances your awareness during movement, fostering a deeper mind-body connection. Joy adds a touch of positivity that infuses both movement and mindfulness with a vibrant energy.

Embodying Wholeness: Your Holistic Lifestyle
As you journey through Chapter 16, envision your life as a canvas—a canvas where movement, mindfulness, and joy create a masterpiece of holistic well-being. These practices are your paintbrushes, crafting a life rich in both physical vitality and emotional flourishing. This chapter empowers you to weave these practices into your daily routine, crafting a lifestyle that embodies wholeness—a lifestyle that reflects your commitment to nurturing your mental health and fostering a resilient mind-body connection.

The Path Forward: A Continual Journey
As you continue to explore the pages of Chapter 16, remember that this is not an endpoint; it's a continuation. The practices of movement, mindfulness, and joy offer an ongoing journey of exploration, growth, and self-discovery. This chapter encourages you to approach these practices with curiosity, embrace the joy they bring, and be patient with the transformation they unfold. By engaging with movement, mindfulness, and joy, you're embarking on a path that transcends limitations and flourishes with the promise of holistic well-being—a path where your mind, body, and spirit thrive in harmonious unity.

Chapter 17: Embracing the Nourished Mindset

Chapter 17 is a profound journey into the realms of self-reflection, gratitude, and the cultivation of a nourished mindset. It's a chapter that transcends the external practices of nutrition, movement, and mindfulness to delve into the internal landscape of your thoughts, beliefs, and attitudes. This chapter is an exploration of how your relationship with food, well-being, and yourself has transformed, and how you can continue to nurture a positive, sustainable, and compassionate approach to holistic health.

The Power of Self-Reflection
At the heart of Chapter 17 lies the power of self-reflection—an introspective journey that invites you to dive deep into your experiences, challenges, and triumphs. This chapter prompts you to pause and look back at the transformation you've undergone throughout your well-being journey. Through self-reflection, you gain insights into your progress, recognize patterns, and acknowledge the milestones that mark your path. It's a practice that fosters self-awareness and reinforces your commitment to nurturing a nourished mind.

Cultivating Gratitude and Appreciation
Gratitude is a beacon of positivity—a light that illuminates the present moment with appreciation and contentment. Chapter 17 explores the practice of cultivating gratitude as a means to enhance your well-being. By acknowledging the

small victories, the supportive relationships, and the nourishing experiences along the way, you're embracing gratitude as a tool to shift your focus from what's lacking to what's abundant in your life. This practice contributes to a nourished mindset, fostering a positive outlook and emotional resilience.

Transforming Your Relationship with Food

This chapter delves into the transformational journey of your relationship with food. It encourages you to shift from a mindset of restriction, guilt, and rigidity to one of flexibility, balance, and self-compassion. It's about letting go of food as an enemy and embracing it as a source of nourishment, pleasure, and connection. By transforming your relationship with food, you're creating a foundation for long-term well-being that goes beyond just physical health.

Cultivating Body Positivity and Self-Love

Nurturing a nourished mindset involves embracing your body with positivity and self-love. This chapter invites you to embrace your body's uniqueness, respecting it as the vessel that carries you through life's journey. By practicing self-compassion, letting go of unrealistic standards, and focusing on your body's strengths and abilities, you're fostering a healthy body image and cultivating a positive connection with yourself.

Mindful Eating as a Mindset

Mindful eating is not just a practice—it's a mindset that extends beyond mealtimes. This chapter explores the integration of mindful eating principles into your daily life. It's about savoring the textures and flavors of each bite, recognizing hunger and fullness cues, and making intentional choices that align with your well-being goals. Mindful eating is a vehicle to cultivate a nourished mindset by fostering a harmonious relationship with food and yourself.

Embracing the Imperfect Journey
Chapter 17 recognizes that the journey to a nourished mindset is not linear—it's marked by ups and downs, challenges and setbacks. It's about embracing the imperfections as integral parts of the path. This chapter encourages you to approach these moments with self-compassion, understanding that setbacks are not failures but opportunities for growth. By embracing the imperfect journey, you're cultivating resilience and reinforcing your commitment to holistic well-being.

Sustaining Your Nourished Mindset
Sustaining a nourished mindset involves consistency, commitment, and ongoing self-care. This chapter offers practical strategies to integrate the principles of self-reflection, gratitude, transformed relationships, and mindful eating into your daily life. It emphasizes the importance of self-check-ins, regular moments of gratitude, and the continual practice of self-compassion.

Embracing Your Ongoing Transformation
As you journey through Chapter 17, remember that this is not a conclusion—it's an invitation to an ongoing transformation. The practices and reflections in this chapter are seeds that you'll continue to nurture as you move forward. They are tools that empower you to navigate life's challenges, maintain a nourished mindset, and continue evolving on the path of holistic well-being.

A Life of Nourishment and Empowerment
In the pages of Chapter 17, you're painting a portrait—a portrait of a life lived with intention, self-awareness, and empowerment. This chapter is an opportunity to create a narrative that resonates with your values, a narrative that celebrates your growth, and a narrative that inspires others to embark on their own journeys of well-being. By embracing a nourished mindset, you're not just transforming your relationship with food and health; you're embracing a holistic lifestyle that nurtures your mind, body, and spirit— a lifestyle that is a testament to your commitment to holistic well-being.

The Reflective Mirror: Self-Exploration and Growth
At the core of Chapter 17 lies the reflective mirror of self-exploration—a tool that allows you to gaze deeply into your own experiences, thoughts, and emotions. This practice invites you to revisit the journey you've embarked upon, acknowledging the progress you've made, the challenges you've overcome, and the lessons you've learned. As you

reflect, you not only honor your growth but also pave the way for continued evolution.

Gratitude as a Catalyst for Well-Being

Gratitude, the gentle force that radiates positivity, is woven into the fabric of Chapter 17. This chapter guides you in nurturing the practice of gratitude—a practice that shifts your perspective from what's lacking to what's abundant in your life. By acknowledging the blessings, both big and small, you cultivate a sense of contentment and joy. Gratitude becomes the compass guiding you towards a nourished mindset, reminding you to cherish the present moment.

The Nurtured Relationship: Food, Body, and Self

The transformation of your relationship with food, body, and self takes center stage in this chapter. It's an exploration of how you've shifted from external judgments to internal kindness, from rigid rules to intuitive understanding. By embracing a nourished mindset, you celebrate food as fuel, nourishment, and pleasure. Your body becomes a vessel deserving of love and respect, and you recognize your intrinsic worth beyond physical appearance.

Cultivating Self-Love and Body Positivity

Cultivating self-love and body positivity becomes an integral theme in this chapter. It's about dismantling the societal constructs that dictate worth based on appearance and embracing a new narrative—one of self-acceptance and appreciation. Through practices of self-compassion, positive affirmations, and shifting self-talk, you forge a deeper connection with yourself, recognizing that your true essence extends far beyond external attributes.

Mindful Eating as a Lifestyle

Mindful eating transcends the confines of mealtimes—it becomes a lifestyle, a way of interacting with food, and a practice of presence. This chapter encourages you to incorporate mindful eating into every aspect of your day, fostering a harmonious relationship with food and self. Mindful eating serves as a bridge between physical nourishment and emotional satisfaction, allowing you to enjoy food fully while respecting your body's cues.

Resilience Amid Imperfection

Acknowledging imperfection becomes a cornerstone of this chapter. Life is a journey marked by twists, turns, and unforeseen challenges. In these moments, a nourished mindset becomes your anchor. Rather than seeing setbacks as failures, you view them as opportunities for growth. This chapter empowers you to approach difficulties with self-compassion, acknowledging that each stumble is a stepping stone towards resilience.

Sustaining Your Nourished Mindset

Sustaining a nourished mindset involves weaving these practices into the fabric of your daily life. The chapter offers practical strategies—such as journaling, gratitude practices, and self-care rituals—to ensure that your nourished mindset remains a constant presence. It's a commitment to your well-being, a dedication to self-nurturing, and an ongoing journey of empowerment.

A Testament to Your Inner Journey

Chapter 17 is a testament—a living testament to your inner journey of transformation and growth. Through self-reflection, gratitude, a transformed relationship with food and body, and the practice of mindfulness, you're crafting a narrative that speaks to your authentic self. This chapter is an affirmation of your commitment to holistic well-being, an embrace of self-compassion, and an invitation to continue nurturing your nourished mindset.

Continuing the Unfolding Journey

As you immerse yourself in the pages of Chapter 17, remember that this isn't the final destination—it's a milestone on an ongoing journey. The practices, reflections, and lessons within this chapter are threads that will continue to weave through the fabric of your life. Your nourished mindset is a beacon guiding you towards holistic well-being—a well-being that emanates from within, resonates with authenticity, and flourishes as you continue to unfold on the path of self-discovery and empowerment.

Chapter 18: Your Journey Ahead- Charting a Path for Continued Growth and Wellness Beyond the Six Weeks

Chapter 18 is a compass, guiding you towards the horizon of continued growth, wellness, and holistic living. As you near the end of this transformative journey, this chapter extends a bridge, inviting you to step onto the path that lies ahead—a path illuminated by the principles, practices, and insights you've embraced throughout this holistic wellness exploration.

Reflection: Honoring Your Progress

Before charting the journey ahead, this chapter encourages reflection—a moment to honor the progress you've made. Reflect on how far you've come since the beginning of this transformative endeavor. Recognize the shifts in your mindset, your relationship with food, and your overall well-being. By acknowledging your achievements, you infuse your journey with a sense of accomplishment and motivation.

Integration: Weaving the Threads

Chapter 18 emphasizes the importance of integrating the practices you've learned into your daily life. It's about weaving the threads of nutritional consciousness, movement, mindfulness, and joy into the tapestry of your routines. This integration isn't about perfection; it's about consistency and intention. By incorporating these practices into your lifestyle, you're laying the foundation for sustained well-being.

Setting Personal Goals: The Next Chapter

This chapter guides you in setting personal goals that align with your evolving well-being journey. Whether it's deepening your mindfulness practice, exploring new forms of movement, or experimenting with new nutrient-rich recipes, setting goals gives you a roadmap for continued growth. These goals serve as guideposts, reminding you of your intentions and propelling you towards new levels of well-being.

Support Systems: Building Your Tribe

Your well-being journey is not a solitary endeavor; it's a shared experience. This chapter delves into the importance of building a support system—a tribe of individuals who share your values and aspirations. Whether it's joining a wellness community, seeking out like-minded friends, or engaging in online forums, a supportive network provides encouragement, accountability, and a sense of belonging.

Adaptation: Embracing Change

Change is a constant in life, and your well-being journey is no exception. This chapter highlights the necessity of adaptability. As you navigate various life stages, challenges, and opportunities, your practices may need to evolve.

Adaptation isn't a sign of regression; it's a testament to your resilience and commitment to well-being.

Sustainable Habits: The Pillars of Well-Being
Sustainability is a pillar of holistic well-being. This chapter underscores the importance of cultivating sustainable habits—practices that are nourishing and enjoyable over the long term. Fad diets and extreme regimens often lead to burnout; sustainable habits, on the other hand, become integral components of your lifestyle, fostering lasting health and vitality.

The Ripple Effect: Inspiring Others
Your well-being journey has the power to inspire those around you. This chapter explores the ripple effect—the idea that your transformation can positively influence your loved ones, friends, and even strangers. By embodying well-being principles, you become a living example of the transformative potential that lies within each individual.

Continuing Education: The Pursuit of Knowledge
Learning is a lifelong endeavor, and this chapter encourages the pursuit of knowledge. Whether it's staying informed about nutritional advancements, deepening your understanding of movement practices, or exploring new mindfulness techniques, continued education enriches your well-being journey and empowers you to make informed choices.

Celebrating Milestones: The Joy of Progress
As you traverse the journey ahead, remember to celebrate milestones—both big and small. Each step forward is a cause for celebration, an opportunity to acknowledge your growth and embrace the joy of progress. Celebrations are not just about reaching the destination; they're about embracing the richness of the journey itself.

A Reflective Pause: Honoring the Distance Traveled
Before embarking on the journey ahead, Chapter 18 invites you to take a reflective pause—a moment to look back at the distance you've traveled since your first step into this well-being exploration. The changes you've witnessed, the breakthroughs you've experienced, and the insights you've gained all deserve recognition. This reflective exercise sets the tone for what's to come—an empowered continuation of your well-being journey.

Seamless Integration: Weaving Well-Being into Life
Integration is the key to lasting change, and this chapter emphasizes the seamless weaving of well-being practices into the fabric of your daily life. The culmination of the preceding chapters has equipped you with a toolkit for holistic living. Now, it's about making these practices second nature. Whether it's mindful eating, incorporating movement, or embracing joy, the more effortlessly these practices integrate, the more profound their impact becomes.

Personal Goals: Pioneering the Uncharted
As you gaze into the horizon of your well-being journey, Chapter 18 encourages you to set personal goals that align with your evolving aspirations. These goals serve as the compass directing your next steps. Whether it's cultivating a deeper mindfulness practice, conquering a fitness milestone, or exploring new culinary territories, personal goals provide direction and purpose.

The Power of Support: Building a Tribe
No journey is solitary, and well-being is no exception. This chapter illuminates the importance of building a supportive tribe—a community of like-minded individuals who share your commitment to holistic living. Whether you find this community in local meetups, virtual forums, or wellness groups, the shared journey creates a support system that uplifts, motivates, and keeps you accountable.

Embracing Adaptability: Navigating Change
Change is the heartbeat of life, and your well-being journey will undoubtedly encounter its rhythm. Chapter 18 reminds you of the importance of adaptability. Life's seasons, circumstances, and priorities shift, and your practices may need to adapt accordingly. This fluidity is not a compromise but a testament to your resilience and your commitment to a well-rounded life.

Sustainability as a Keystone: Cultivating Habits that Last

Sustainability is the cornerstone of well-being and longevity. This chapter underscores the significance of cultivating sustainable habits—practices that align with your values, support your health, and bring you joy. These habits are not fleeting trends but enduring companions that contribute to a flourishing life.

Inspiration in Action: Ripples of Impact

Your journey is not just personal; it's also a source of inspiration for those around you. Chapter 18 delves into the concept of the ripple effect—how your transformation can catalyze positive change in your community. By embodying well-being principles, you set an example that has the potential to motivate others to embark on their own journeys of transformation.

Lifelong Learning: Nourishing the Mind

The pursuit of knowledge is an eternal river that enriches your well-being journey. Chapter 18 encourages you to engage in ongoing education—continuing to explore nutritional advancements, deepening your movement practices, and discovering new mindfulness techniques. This commitment to learning empowers you to make informed choices that align with your evolving well-being goals.

Celebrate Your Journey: Joy in Every Step

Celebration is a vital part of your well-being narrative. Each milestone, breakthrough, and instance of growth deserves celebration. Chapter 18 invites you to celebrate the journey itself—the joy of progress, the resilience in challenges, and the beauty of embracing well-being. Celebrations become markers that fuel your motivation and amplify your sense of achievement.

Uncharted Horizons: The Story Continues
As you close the chapter on this transformative odyssey, remember that Chapter 18 is not an end but a prelude to the chapters yet unwritten. Your journey is a canvas that you'll continue to paint with choices, experiences, and growth. The pages of your well-being story are vast, waiting to be filled with the vibrant colors of health, vitality, and fulfillment. As you step into this uncharted terrain, know that your journey toward holistic well-being is a lifelong adventure—an adventure that will continue to empower, inspire, and nurture you every step of the way.

Conclusion- Embracing the Symphony of Well-Being

As we stand on the threshold of closing the chapter on this remarkable voyage, it's a moment to pause and reflect on the journey we've undertaken together through the pages of "Nourishing the Mind: A 6-Week Journey to Overcome Depression and Anxiety." This isn't just the end of a book; it's a new beginning—a prologue to a life transformed by resilience, empowered by knowledge, and enriched by holistic well-being.

From the very first word to the final chapter, this book has been an exploration—an exploration into the interwoven realms of nutrition, psychology, mindfulness, and self-discovery. It's been a journey that transcends the mere act of reading words on a page; it's been an odyssey that invited you to become an active participant, a co-creator in the symphony of your own well-being.

Imagine this book as a symphony, each chapter a movement, each page a note, and each word a brushstroke on the canvas of your mind. Together, they compose a harmonious melody—a melody of knowledge, empowerment, and transformation. Just as a symphony is brought to life by a conductor and performed by an orchestra, your well-being journey is guided by your choices and brought to life through your actions.

From the Science of Nutritional Psychiatry to the exploration of essential nutrients, the nurturing of neurogenesis, the dance of gut-brain harmony, and the crafting of mood-boosting plates, each chapter has been a thread in the tapestry of your well-being. It's a tapestry woven not just from words, but from intentions, commitment, and a burning desire to rise above the challenges that depression and anxiety may have presented.

Throughout these pages, you've encountered the healing power of food—the notion that your plate is not merely a source of sustenance, but a canvas for the art of self-care. You've learned that what you choose to nourish your body with has a profound impact on your mind, and that the act of mindful eating can be a transformative practice that bridges the gap between emotional well-being and physical health.

As you journeyed through each week, you explored the realms of self-compassion, nutrient-rich nourishment, mindful cooking rituals, emotional resilience through movement, and the delicate dance of mind-body harmony. Each step has been an invitation to reconnect with yourself, rediscover the joy in movement, embrace the art of cooking as an act of love, and cultivate a mindset that empowers you to navigate life's ebbs and flows.

But this book isn't just a collection of practices and principles; it's an invitation to become the author of your own well-being narrative—a narrative that goes beyond the confines of these pages and extends into the tapestry of your life. The seeds of knowledge you've sown, the practices you've embraced, and the wisdom you've gleaned are meant to flourish beyond these words, inspiring you to create a life that's rooted in resilience, nourished by self-care, and fueled by purpose.

As you close this chapter, remember that the journey doesn't end here—it continues with each mindful bite, each intentional breath, and each step you take toward holistic well-being. The lessons you've learned, the recipes you've discovered, and the habits you've cultivated are tools in your well-being arsenal—tools that will serve you not just in times of challenge, but in moments of joy, celebration, and ongoing growth.

The title "Nourishing the Mind" is a testament to your commitment, your courage, and your resilience. It's a reminder that the journey towards overcoming depression and anxiety is a journey towards reclaiming your power, your joy, and your sense of self. You are not defined by your struggles, but by the strength with which you rise above them.

So, as you close this chapter, know that you hold within you the echoes of empowerment, the whispers of self-care, and the promise of a future that's illuminated by well-being. Your journey is not just a 6-week endeavor; it's an eternal dance—a symphony that will continue to evolve, resonate, and inspire the harmonious melody of your life. As the conductor of your own symphony, remember that the power to nourish your mind, overcome challenges, and embrace joy is always within your grasp. The stage is set, and the music is yours to create.

<u>Check and read other books by Jerry Clarke on amazon</u>